NINE LIVES

Absolute Abundance!

Mary Can

NINE LIVES ═══════

Stories of Women Business Owners
Landing on Their Feet

by MARY CANTANDO
with LAURIE ZUCKERMAN

C&A

Cantando & Associates, LLC
Raleigh, North Carolina

Cantando & Associates, LLC
Raleigh, North Carolina
www.WomanBusinessOwner.com

ISBN 0-9729528-0-2

First paperback edition July 2003

Text design by Hannah Lerner
Cover design by Cindy LaBreacht

This book is printed on acid-free paper and
manufactured in the United States of America.

1   2   3   4   5   6   7   8   9   10

CONTENTS

FOREWORD

WOMEN IN THE PAST CENTURY have made magnificent strides. Nowhere is this more apparent than in the exponential growth in the number of women business owners. While the number of women CEOs at Fortune companies remains painfully low, women in the United States are starting businesses at twice the rate of men. In corporate salary surveys, women continue to lag well behind men in every category. In fact, the only marketplace where women's compensation is equal to that of men is among business owners. Women business owners pay themselves at the same level as their male counterparts.

But financials alone should not be our barometer of success; nor should accumulation of titles, of customers or of board positions. The women in this book are magnificent—not because of what they have accumulated or even because of what they have accomplished—but because of who they have become. Each woman, through her business, has experienced an epiphany, an awakening, a newfound sense of self.

These powerful stories, in turn, encourage each of us to seek our own new sense of self, whether the route is a return to school, a step up the corporate ladder or the founding of a new business. These nine women have followed their dreams. They inspire us to do the same.

MARSHA FIRESTONE, PH.D.
President, The Women Presidents' Organization

THIS BOOK IS DEDICATED to women in business everywhere. May your bright light illuminate the path for future generations.

∼

A SINCERE THANK YOU to the magnificent women profiled in this book. Their wisdom is a special gift to us all and we're grateful for the difference they're making in the world.

Thanks also to the organizations that support women business owners. It is an honor to participate with you and share your vision of enabling a vital environment for women entrepreneurs across the country.

And finally, thanks to our families and the families of the women profiled in this book. Your continued encouragement allows us to pursue lives that others only dream of.

PREFACE

IN SEPTEMBER OF 2002, I sat in a boardroom in Plano, Texas with some of the most remarkable women in the world. As I glanced around the table, my eyes met those of a woman who had started a manufacturing plant in Kentucky to provide jobs to a community with drastically high unemployment; the CEO of the only woman-owned business ever to trade on NASDAQ; a woman who developed a for-profit company that only hires people with disabilities; a woman who had left Iran as a teen-ager and now owns a multimillion dollar technology firm, and on and on.

The firepower of the women in that room was astounding. It occurred to me that if I could somehow capture the wisdom in that room, women across the country would benefit. So I approached several of these women and asked them to provide me with their two most precious commodities: their time and their history. The stories they shared were awe inspiring, funny, mind boggling . . . and sometimes painful. There were tough moments when the women opened up about still-raw details of their pasts. They had to overcome natural urges to protect their privacy and to hide from memories that they'd just as soon forget. Seeing those details put down on paper was even more excruciating for some of them. Yet, time and again, these brave women said that they were willing to swallow their discomfort if other women could learn from or be inspired by their struggles.

Each of these women has a one-of-a-kind gift. And each has overcome her own personal set of obstacles. Any sane person would have bet money against any of them becoming even mildly successful. Yet, against these odds, a passion bubbled up, allowing each to tap into her strength and make a real difference in the world.

Many of the women in this book are members of two highly regarded national organizations with which I'm proud to be affiliated. The Women Presidents' Organization (WPO) is a national non-profit consisting of women from across the country whose companies each generate at least $2 million in annual revenue. The Women's Business Enterprise National Council (WBENC) is the most highly regarded third-party certifying organization of women-owned businesses in the United States. These organizations have put me in touch with some of the most spectacular people I've ever met. I hope that by sharing the stories of a few of these women, I am in some small way returning the favor.

MARY CANTANDO

NINE LIVES ═══════════

A SEAT AT THE TABLE

REBECCA BOENIGK

CEO, Neutral Posture, Inc.
Bryan, Texas

R ACHEL, AGE THIRTEEN, couldn't wait to show her mom the great game her Texas history teacher had introduced to her class. As soon as Rachel got home, she plugged the CD-ROM into her PC and yelled for Rebecca. "See," she said to her mom, slowly moving the mouse across the map of Texas. "It's a commodities game. You get to drive all over Texas and you figure out where to buy stuff in different places."

Rebecca asked if she could give it a try. Rachel shifted so her mom could take control of the mouse. Rebecca directed the mouse straight to the city of Bryan.

"Rachel, look at this. In Bryan, you buy furniture. That's us! That's Neutral Posture."

"Wow!" Rachel said. "But how do they know you are there?"

"Because we have to pay taxes to the state of Texas and it shows that we are in the furniture business."

Rachel went back to school, grinning from ear to ear, and told her teacher that her mom's company was on the CD-ROM. Everyone in the class loved the idea that they could go to Bryan and buy furniture from Rachel's mom.

~

When Rebecca Boenigk was thirteen, she never would have imagined that she would someday own a successful furniture company. Not to say she wasn't a pretty confident kid. She was. Her mother had drilled it into her head from infancy that she could do anything she wanted to do, be anything she wanted to be. "Never accept second best," she had told her daughter at every opportunity. Once, when five-year-old Rebecca was playing hospital with friends, her mother overheard Rebecca volunteering to be the nurse. Her mother rushed into the room. "You don't have to be the nurse just because you are a girl, you can be the doctor!" she said.

Well, Rebecca never had the least interest in becoming a doctor. Throughout her school days, she actually had no idea what she wanted to do. She figured that someday she'd just go out, get a job and pull in a big paycheck.

As it turned out, getting jobs was something at which she was pretty good. As Rebecca saw it, school was a bit of a bore. What she really liked was making money. At fourteen, it was a job at Dairy Queen—the only place that would hire her. At sixteen, she was working as a dental assistant.

During Rebecca's sophomore year of high school, her father's company transferred him from Texas to Indiana. Now, moving was something the Congleton family happened to know a lot about. Until Rebecca's father, Jerome Congleton, began working in private industry, he had been a career military man. A Vietnam veteran with 213 combat missions under his belt, Jerome flew for seven years as a fighter pilot in the United States Air Force. His military career had uprooted the family countless times. They'd even spent four years living in Germany. Moving had never bothered Rebecca before. But then again, she had never before known what it was to feel at home. Texas felt like home.

Rebecca never did adjust to life in Indiana. After bearing up for a little over a year, she realized that though only a junior, she had enough credits to graduate from high school. She was going back to Texas.

Rebecca's parents, missing Texas themselves, decided to join her. Jerome left his job and enrolled in graduate studies. He and his daughter walked onto Texas Tech University together for their first day of school in 1981. Rebecca was a seventeen-year-old sophomore—her high SAT scores had placed her out of freshman year. Jerome was a thirty-eight-year-old Ph.D. candidate studying ergonomic engineering.

College was a little overwhelming for Rebecca. Though her parents lived in town, she lived in the dorms to get the full college experience. But she was a good deal younger and less experienced than her classmates. It was reassuring to meet up with her father for an occasional lunch.

In her second semester, Rebecca became Jerome's research assistant. She was initially attracted to the flexible hours, but she soon became fascinated by her father's research. Jerome had worked at Alcoa for eight years as an industrial engineer and safety manager. The more he dug into safety-related issues at the corporation, the more clearly he began to see that many job-related injuries could be relieved and even prevented by office chairs that protected—not injured—the back. Now, in the 1980s, ergonomics was not a word you often heard. This revolutionary idea captured Jerome's imagination.

At Texas Tech, Jerome researched the position that an astronaut assumes while sleeping in a weightless environment in outer space—free, natural and without stress. The position shows the body completely relaxed with the muscles, tendons and ligaments in balance and the vertebrae equally spaced. The chair that Jerome designed as part of his research supported the body in this natural position. As a result of this support, the muscle system becomes non-stressed; the discs in the vertebrae align properly; breathing, digestion, and circulation improve while tension and discomfort from stress and fatigue are virtually eliminated. This all made perfect sense to him.

After two years, Jerome received his Doctorate of Philosophy in Industrial Engineering with a research emphasis in ergonomics/human factors. He was then hired to teach at Texas A&M in College Station. Over the same time period, Rebecca transferred to the University of Texas in Austin to study communications. Again, school failed to challenge her and hold her attention. She worked part time as a bank teller and part time managing an apartment complex. She told her father that she wanted to drop out of college and just work. He told her no. She stayed in school, but started going to fewer and fewer classes. Finally, at age twenty, she quit. She didn't know what she wanted to do, but she was clear on one thing, college wasn't for her.

～

Meanwhile, at College Station, Jerome was caught up in some pretty interesting discussions about the ergonomic chair he had developed for his dissertation. Texas A&M had a program called INVENT (Institute for Ventures in New Technology) designed to help professors commercialize their products. Did Jerome want to work with the university to start a company to take his chair to market?

Some intense family discussions followed. The outgrowth: Congleton Workplace Systems, owned sixty percent by the Congletons, fifteen percent by Texas A&M and twenty-five percent by other investors. The startup team consisted of the Congleton family: Jerome, his wife, his daughter and his son, a recent college graduate. The company was assigned a team of Texas A&M professors to serve as advisors.

Rebecca was in charge of the facility. She also continued to work with her father in research & development and served as the liaison with the parts vendors. Rebecca's mother, Jaye Congleton, handled the accounting. Her brother handled sales.

The business started during a rough period for Texans. Every day seemed to bring another headline of a bank going under. Venture capital was basically nonexistent. The family struggled to drum up sales and get the business going. And then finally, just when Congleton Workplace Systems had gotten on its feet and started filling purchase orders, the business ran out of money. They couldn't buy parts to fill their orders. They couldn't meet payroll. And with the state's banks in sorry shape, they couldn't find anyone to give them capital. They were stuck. In the summer of 1988, the Congletons declared personal bankruptcy, went through SBA foreclosure and shut down.

"Why? Why? How could this happen?" was the wail pervading the Congleton house over the next few weeks. They had put their faith in the counsel that their advisors, the team of A&M professors, had offered. The advisors had earned Ph.D.'s in economics. They were people who should know who was who and what was what. The trouble was that the professors knew theories. They knew numbers. They did not seem to grasp realities. The professors kept telling them to invest, invest, invest in their business. They kept looking down the road two years, four years, six years. Meanwhile, the Congletons couldn't meet payroll.

The day that the company's business assets were tagged for auction, Rebecca wandered around the office crying her eyes out. They had worked so hard to finally get the business going. It would all be lost. It all had been for nothing. The assets, representing almost four years of their lives, sold for $11,000.

∾

Though her career was in shambles, one thing was going right in twenty-four-year-old Rebecca's life. Three days prior to the foreclosure auction, her boyfriend, Bobby Boenigk, had proposed. Rebecca was ready with a quick answer. Seven weeks earlier, after their very first date, she came home and told her mother, "That is the man I am going to marry."

"Yeah, right," Jaye responded. Her daughter was infamous for her string of week-long romances. But this was different. This was true love. Bobby and Rebecca understood each other. Eight weeks after the couple's engagement, just fifteen weeks after their first date, the happy couple became husband and wife.

7

But when the excitement of the wedding started to fade, Rebecca fell into a deep depression. Just getting up in the morning took too much energy to muster. She lay around in a yellow bathrobe hashing over what had gone wrong, trying to imagine what she could do with her life that could possibly match the excitement of starting a business. She wondered whether anyone would even hire her again. Her self-esteem was shot.

One morning, she told herself to just pull it together already. She would be a housewife and eventually a stay-at-home mom and it would be okay. She would make it okay. However, after three months of cooking beautiful dinners, vacuuming the rugs, dusting her china and watching a lot of TV, Rebecca realized she was fooling herself. She was bored and unhappy and it wasn't okay. But she knew how to fix it.

In December, Rebecca sat down with her husband and her parents. "We can start the business again by ourselves," she said. "We obviously know how *not* to do it. We can't stop now. Let's give it a whirl."

Though they had confidence in themselves, the banks didn't. The Congleton's poor credit rating sent financial institutions running. Vendors were equally clear: no up-front payments, no parts. So Bobby borrowed $20,000 from his employer and Jerome kicked in another $30,000 he had received in consulting fees. They were on their way.

In January 1989, Neutral Posture was incorporated. This time it was just Rebecca and her mother working full-time out of Rebecca's garage. Jerome, still a professor at Texas A&M, served as research & development consultant. Rebecca was the chairman of the board. Jaye handled the bookkeeping and Rebecca handled the sales. They manufactured the chairs together. Jaye built the backrests while her daughter built the seats.

Jaye had no problem letting her young daughter grab the reins of the company. It made sense. As she saw it, ever since

Rebecca had turned three, the spunky toddler had been her boss. "Mommy, you are washing the dishes wrong," and "Mommy, that's not how to vacuum," she would say. No doubt, Rebecca knew what was what.

And now mother and daughter both knew what was what about how to make a business succeed. There was very little stress in those early days. The worst had already happened; they knew what it was like to fail. In control of their own business, they proved that they had learned their lessons well. They didn't spend any money that they didn't have. They didn't even draw a salary for the first two years. By the end of their first year, they did, however, make enough in sales to pay back the money they had borrowed.

One of Neutral Posture's first big breaks came when a New Orleans newspaper, on the brink of ordering 150 new office chairs, selected the company as one of five chair makers to compete in a sit-down competition. Neutral Posture's chair— the only one they could muster up on such short notice—was emblazoned with the Texas A&M logo. The test chairs were arranged in a conference room and groups of five employees at a time were encouraged to sit for several minutes in each of the five contenders. "I want the Aggie chair," was the rallying cry, and this was in Louisiana State University country. Ninety-seven out of the first 100 people chose the Neutral Posture chair.

All told, it was an eventful first year. Day by day, the business grew bigger—and so did Rebecca. Just one month into the new business, Rebecca and Bobby decided to start a family. Rebecca figured she had already done this crazy thing of starting another business, so why not just go all out? A month later, she was pregnant.

Her daughter, Rachel, was born in December of 1989. Just ten days later, Rebecca was back at work. Newborn Rachel simply became a part of the Neutral Posture team. Mother, daughter and granddaughter all went out on sales calls together.

Jaye usually stayed back in the mini-van with Rachel while Rebecca knocked on doors.

In February of 1990, Neutral Posture moved out of Rebecca's garage and into an 8,000-square-foot building. Compared to the family garage, the space was overwhelming. Even little Rachel had her own office, well equipped with a crib, a high chair and a wide assortment of toys. At nine months old, Rachel, proving that the apple didn't fall far from the tree, managed to evade her caregivers and take off running. Ensconced in her walker, she crossed the production floor, traversed the parking lot and fell into a ditch. The very next day, the baby found herself in day care.

Rebecca and Jaye manufactured the first 1,500 chairs with their own two hands. A little over a year after beginning production, when business had picked up, they made their first hires. Their timing was perfect. Rebecca was pregnant again. But this pregnancy was different. The nausea began when she was three weeks along and continued throughout the rest of the pregnancy. Leaning over a swollen stomach to screw bolts into chairs just didn't have much appeal.

Baby Ryan was born in September of 1991. Eight weeks early, he weighed two pounds, ten ounces. He was tiny. And perfect.

While recovering in the hospital from her delivery, Rebecca rejoiced in her son's teeny fingers and toes. She stroked his fuzzy grapefruit head. She also closed her first deal with Intel Corporation. Rebecca kept her very recent delivery strictly out of her phone conversations with the computing giant. She didn't want to entertain any suggestions about holding off until she felt better. She wanted that contract closed. Bobby brought the papers to the hospital to sign. And so Rebecca brought home from the hospital a new baby and her business' most important contract to date.

Intel's first order was for 100 chairs specifically designated for employees with medical conditions. How many bad backs could there be? Intel figured these 100 chairs would be enough to last them a year. They were wrong. All the chairs were snapped up within nine days. It was a wake-up call for Intel. Rather than thinking of the chairs as "band-aids" for people who already had medical issues, they decided to take a more proactive route. They would start an ergonomics program geared at preventing carpel tunnel injuries to wrists and the many other upper body, neck, and shoulder disorders that can occur when office workers spend upwards of six hours a day at their computers. Intel decided to give every office worker his or her own ergonomic chair. Was Neutral Posture big enough to handle it? Sure, Rebecca responded.

A few days later Rebecca got a call from Intel that a purchase order was about to come through. She walked over and stood by the fax, clenching her hands in anticipation. She had no idea what the order would be. Slowly the paper rolled through the machine. Rebecca grabbed it up as soon as it cleared the roller. She scanned the page quickly: 700 chairs. "Oh my goodness!" she screamed, jumping up and down.

Then the next purchase order came. And the next. All told, Intel wanted 2,300 chairs in ninety days. Rebecca panicked. At this point, Neutral Posture had thirty employees and was manufacturing about 500 chairs a month. Their average sale was 2.5 chairs. Rebecca called an emergency meeting with her mother, her husband and David Ebner, her plant manager. "What are we going to do?" she asked, her brown eyes wild in her pale face.

"We are going to make those chairs," David responded.

Neutral Posture hired a small army of temporary workers. The new people were teamed with the company's most experienced employees. In the end, 2,300 chairs were delivered on time and in perfect condition. Neutral Posture had pulled it off.

David was not surprised. "We specialize in the impossible," was the motto he had brought to the company, and their success in this specialty paid off. Over the next three years, Intel bought another 9,000 chairs from Neutral Posture.

Over time, Rebecca got even better at making the sale. Instead of targeting the facilities people, she learned that the best way into a company was often through the back door. The health and safety people understood the rationale of paying more for an ergonomic chair. They understood that the inexpensive chairs that locked employees into a less-than-ideal position for hours at a time could easily result in a greater number of injuries and cost them more over time in higher insurance bills.

Purchase orders, averaging 2.5 chairs per order, continued to trickle in. Then, in 1994, Rebecca got a call from United Parcel Services. The company was interested in purchasing 1,100 chairs for a new corporate office in Atlanta. Rebecca was thrilled. She flew to Atlanta and met with the purchasing director. As Rebecca talked about the features and benefits of Neutral Posture's chairs, the director's eyes lit up. He began thumbing through his file, noting more and more locations that needed chairs. As he talked, Rebecca sat across the conference table from him, nodding her head where warranted and frantically trying to add up numbers. Finally, the meeting came to an end and the UPS director handed Rebecca a handwritten purchase order. With the PO in hand, she shook the director's hand, stood up and walked out of the room.

Outside the meeting room, Rebecca leaned up against a wall for support. She looked at the PO again: 7,200 chairs. It was way beyond her company's production capabilities. But they would deliver them somehow. And with the help of temporary workers and a lot of sweat and creativity, they did it again—7,200 chairs, on time and in perfect condition. Once more, the reward proved worth the effort. All told, over the next ten years, UPS purchased another 30,000 chairs from Neutral Posture.

By 1996, Neutral Posture had outgrown the 8,000-square-foot site that Rebecca, in 1991, had wailed would never be filled. They'd found a 50,000-square-foot building to purchase. Backed by a seven-year track record and sales in excess of $12 million, Rebecca and Jaye knew they would have no problem securing a loan. When they arranged the financing, they told the banker that the two of them would guarantee the loan. But when it came time to close on the building, the bank had instead listed their husbands, Jerome and Bobby, as guarantors. Rebecca and Jaye were appalled. "That is just the way we do it," the women were told.

"Can you prove to us that the businessmen who come into this bank have to get their wives to co-sign their loans?" Jaye demanded. The bankers hemmed and hawed. The papers were redrawn.

Rebecca and Jaye believed in standing their ground. And as the years passed, they came to better understand just exactly where that ground lay. Rebecca's business ethics were tested in 1997 when a customer, Lockheed Martin, ordered 3,568 chairs. Rebecca realized that if the buyer increased the order by just thirty-two chairs, the order would be placed in the next price category, lowering the price on all the chairs and essentially giving Lockheed Martin 200 free chairs. Rebecca and her team considered not coming forth with this information. Then Rebecca had a conversation with her husband. There was only one choice, Bobby told her: she had to tell the buyer. After all, what kind of relationship did she want to have with her customers? Rebecca slowly nodded her head. She called the buyer to personally explain the situation. He was blown away by that phone call. The buyer couldn't believe the company would be so up front. But he didn't change the order. As it turned out, each employee had individually picked the chair he or she wanted and the buyer didn't need any more chairs.

Nevertheless, the call was far from wasted. That conversation cemented a relationship of trust with Lockheed Martin that culminated in more orders for many thousands of chairs. And for Neutral Posture, a standard was established: honesty and openness would dictate all their business dealings. Their new motto: "While sitting is our foundation, it is what we stand for that counts."

~

The business grew faster than Rebecca and her mother would have dared to dream possible. In 1995 and 1996, Neutral Posture was listed by *Inc* magazine in its annual *Inc 500*, a list of the nation's fastest growing private companies. Rebecca and Jaye were recipients of the 1997 Ernst & Young Entrepreneur of the Year Award for Manufacturing for the Houston Region. They were thrilled.

But someone else was not. The businessman who had purchased the assets of the Congleton's first business sued Neutral Posture again and again. It hardly surprised Rebecca that he was unhappy to see such a formidable competitor rise from the ashes, but she couldn't fathom his venomous reaction. She felt like she was being entangled in a sticky web of litigation by a weird shadow of her former business. When this competitor decided to go public, Rebecca felt that in order to compete effectively she had little choice but to follow suit.

And there was some glamour to the idea. The market for IPOs was thriving in 1997 and newspapers brimmed with accounts of everyday entrepreneurs striking it big in the public market. With visions of her company's name on the NASDAQ stock ticker, Rebecca loved every minute of the IPO process. She had no problem finding an underwriter willing to place all of Neutral Posture's stock, and the consequent road show was as exciting and productive as she had hoped. And so, on October 21, 1997, Neutral Posture started trading on the NASDAQ stock exchange under the call letters NTRL.

That very day, as the excitement unfolded, Rebecca was on a plane driving David, her plant manager, nuts. Like a kid stuck in bed on Christmas morning, Rebecca wiggled nervously around in her seat. She picked up the phone over and over to call in and get the stock quote: "Did it go up? Did it go up?" The stock hovered at around six dollars.

Three days later, Neutral Posture's closing meeting was held. It was official: Rebecca became the CEO of the only woman-owned business trading on NASDAQ.

The company celebrated at a huge closing party in Dallas. Clutching a glass of champagne, Rebecca reveled in her company's success. She thought of all the companies who wanted to go public, but could never quite get to that level. She couldn't believe they had really pulled it off. Her little company was an official part of the stock ticker.

The party marked the best moment that Rebecca would experience as the head of a publicly traded company. The next week, she met the company's new outside board of directors. Each board member had at least twenty years of experience and a few college degrees on Rebecca. Each board member had some very strong opinions which he or she didn't mind sharing—loudly.

For the first time in the nine years since she had started the business, Rebecca lived with the taste of anxiety in her mouth. Some nights she would go home and cry on her husband's shoulder: They keep telling me how to do things. They don't respect me or my decisions. They don't understand the business. They don't get what it will take to move the business to the next level. They are going to make us fail.

Rebecca got to the point where she felt like no matter what she proposed, the board was going to fight her every step of the way. But some battles are worth fighting. When she told the board she wanted to buy the assets of another chair company, the board gave her ninety different reasons why that wasn't going to happen and wouldn't be successful. The logic didn't make sense to Rebecca. One of the driving reasons she had become a public company was to have the means to acquire other businesses. In this case, she had enough cash to make the buy. So she would go for it.

She had first caught wind of the deal in January 1998 from one of her reps in New York. He suggested that Neutral Posture plug a gap in its product line by purchasing the assets of bankrupt Harvard Interiors. The purchase would give reps a line of quality, lower priced products with which to woo the middle market. Rebecca put a bid of $600,000 in with the bankruptcy court. Then another bidder entered the picture. The sale would ultimately come down to a phone auction.

Rebecca sat down with her team to discuss how high they should go in the auction. After some debate, they decided to each write down a number. The range went from $1.3 million to $1.8 million. To no one's surprise, Rebecca had scribbled the highest number.

On the day of the auction, Rebecca, Jaye, David and the CFO gathered around the conference phone. An avid auction-goer, Rebecca was in a state of nervous excitement. The rest of her team was just plain scared. They had seen Rebecca in action at auctions before. They knew losing did not come easily to their intrepid CEO. They held their breath.

The auctioneer set the rules of the auction. Bidding would start at $600,000. Would the bidders be willing to go up in $25,000 increments? "Sure," Rebecca piped in. A voice over the phone requested they move up in $10,000 increments. Rebecca sat back in her chair and grinned at her team. She knew right then that she would win.

The bidding began. The other side threw in a bid of $610,000; Rebecca quickly countered with $620,000. At $660,000 Rebecca began to hear hesitation on the other end. She refused to let any note of uncertainty be detected in her voice. She was there to play ball and she wanted them to know it. At $740,000, a soft voice came through the conference phone, "We are done."

Rebecca was barely able to contain herself as they wrapped up logistics on the call. Finally, assuming the call was over, she bounded up and ran yelling down the hall, "We won! We won!" She was mortified to learn later that day that the businessmen, still on the line, had heard her and burst into laughter. However, they were gentlemen. A tremendous bouquet of roses arrived from Rebecca's contenders the very next day.

Neutral Posture immediately sold off $150,000 of Harvard's assets. The rest was loaded up into fifty-three tractor trailers and put into a leased 10,000-square-foot building. In less than fourteen days, the Harvard line of chairs was available for sale. Over the next five years, the product line brought in $20 million in sales.

The success of the Harvard purchase was yet another indication to Rebecca that her board was just plain giving her bad advice. At the same time, even as Neutral Posture's sales soared from $12 million to $17 million, their stock soured. It slowly sank from six dollars to around a dollar. Clearly, the business was undervalued in the public market. Rebecca could no longer see what being publicly held was buying her company. The cost alone for all the accounting, legal, and reporting work they needed just to comply with the regulations for public companies was upwards of $250,000 a year. After four years as a public company, Rebecca and Jaye decided to break free of their chains.

Rebecca told the board of directors—in politer words than she would have liked to have used—that she wanted out. She would take the company private again. At that point, the board separated from the company and become strictly representative of the shareholders. They hired a firm to evaluate the company and come up with a fair market price. In April 2001, Rebecca and Jaye took the company private at a cost of $2.27 a share, a total of about $3 million. The average purchase price for those still holding stocks was about $1.75, so the majority of the remaining stockholders walked away happy after receiving a premium on the stock.

Rebecca was the happiest of all. She had her business back. It was an incredible feeling. Only in her nightmares would she ever see the faces of some of her board members again.

∼

The very first thing Rebecca did as a newly privately held company was to throw out the business dress code her board had forced on the company. She had thought it was ridiculous from day one. In Neutral Posture's production facility, no one just dropped by. Customer visits were a planned event, and Rebecca wanted her employees to feel comfortable at work. Jeans, shorts and t-shirts once again became standard fare.

Next, Rebecca implemented the benefits that her board had shot down. She set up a matching 401K plan and reinstated the old profit-sharing program for her employees—ideas that provided terrific incentives for employees, but ones that the board had thrown out as unfair to the shareholders. The quarterly profit-sharing plan, for example, is distributed out equally among all employees. Rebecca's check is written for the same amount as the check of the person who packs chairs in boxes. This sends two important messages to employees. First, no one person is more important than anyone else. Second, cost-cutting puts more cash in everyone's pocket. Rebecca found that profit-sharing helped employees start looking at their processes—and the company—very differently.

Rebecca also continued the long-held tradition of buying school supplies for all of her employees' kids—a perk that the employees loved and the board had rejected as "silly." These were changes that made a significant difference to the way employees looked at their jobs. Company morale improved dramatically.

Meanwhile, the mood of Rebecca, Jaye and all the executives was downright euphoric. They were finally freed from the public market fixation on the here and now. They could do what they had wanted to do all along: base decisions on what would be right for the company rather than on what would help the company look the best in the following quarter. One big decision that made sense for the long-term health of the company was to open a new facility near Toronto, Canada. They needed the manufacturing muscle to continue growing, many of their vendors were located in the region and the exchange rate worked in Neutral Posture's favor. Had they still been a public company, Neutral Posture would have been slaughtered for the expense.

The move from private to public to private again reinforced another lesson. No longer would Rebecca play defensive. She had pursued an IPO, in large part, because her litigious competitor had made the first move. He'd gone public and she'd felt she had to follow suit. Rebecca didn't want to play follow-the-leader—or any game—with her competitors anymore. From now on, she'd play by her own rules and be directed by her own vision for her company.

It made all the difference. At a time when all of her competitors, many of them multi-billion-dollar businesses, were aiming their sights solely at the big contracts, Rebecca was focusing her efforts on providing excellent customer service to every customer—large and small. Now that's not to say she turned away General Electric when an order came in for 100 chairs, but she also made sure that all of her employees and reps shared a philosophy that the mom and pop shop with an order of three chairs was just as important to the company's success as were the business giants.

With that mindset, when the economy tumbled, Neutral Posture didn't suffer along with the rest of its industry. Because the company isn't tied to just a few purse strings, Neutral Posture continues to do well, selling about 75,000 chairs each year. While the office furniture industry's revenues have plummeted by fifty percent, Neutral Posture's revenues have remained flat at around $17 million since 2000. Rebecca anticipates that the 2003 revenues of her ninety-five-person company will grow to $20 million.

~

At thirty-nine, Rebecca has had ergonomics on the brain ever since she first signed on as her dad's research assistant at age seventeen. The ever-changing nature of the business continues to fascinate her just as the warm workplace environment she has created embraces her. But lately Rebecca finds her attention turning outward, away from the business. Her family, her church, her community, her network of women business owners—these are the things that earn more and more of her mindshare.

From within her business, Rebecca has always put a focus on her community. In addition to corporate sponsorships and donations to more than 100 charities in the area, Neutral Posture employees are actively encouraged to volunteer. Employees receive one paid day off for every twenty hours of time they donate to churches, schools or other organizations.

But these days, Rebecca is beginning to focus on the community outside of her business. She'd like to semi-retire by age forty-five to devote more time to community work. She finds her talents are in high demand. For one, Rebecca has no compunctions about asking corporations for money to support a worthy cause. Last year, she had an idea for a silent auction to raise money for the Women's Business Enterprise National Council (WBENC), a non-profit certifier of women-owned businesses that helps bring organizations with diversity goals together with qualified women-owned businesses. Rebecca thought the auction was a great idea, but she couldn't drum up much support for it among WBENC's members. They doubted the auction would raise enough money to be worth the effort. So Rebecca pulled it off by herself and single-handedly raised $30,000. This year, with a team of people helping her, including her daughter, Rachel, the auction's goal is to raise $100,000.

As the chair of WBENC's National Women's Enterprise Leadership Forum, Rebecca spends about a quarter of her time on WBENC business. WBENC has helped her open doors to new business like Texas Instruments. Now she wants to give something back to the organization. And she loves it. She's carved out her seat at the table. Now she is helping other women business owners get their chance to break into big business by teaching what she has learned.

The single most important lesson Rebecca feels she's absorbed over the years is about faith—faith in God, faith in her staff and partners and, above all, faith in herself. Too often, she believes, we allow others to make us doubt ourselves. This is not to say that Rebecca believes in ignoring the input of others or in making rash decisions. Quite the opposite, she has a rule that all big decisions must be slept on. And, she's amazed at how often, once she walks away and lets her mind clear, her vision or decision can change. But the most important part of Rebecca's decision-making is that after taking all the input and carefully considering all the angles of an issue she is ultimately guided by her mind, her experience, her vision. Not an advisor's. Not a board member's. Not a competitor's. The call to action is *hers*. And that simple lesson has made all the difference.

THE WOLVES
AT THE DOOR

BARBARA ARMAND
President and CEO, Armand Corporation
Cherry Hill, New Jersey

I T'S NEVER TOO LATE for childhood dreams. That was the lesson Barbara Armand learned at age forty-three when she participatcd in a ceremony that honored her as one of six recipients of the Girl Scouts' Outstanding Woman of Achievement Award. As Barbara recited the Girl Scout oath, the words took her back in time to the days when she was a young girl just dying to join the Girl Scouts.

But black girls in the segregated town of Kentwood, Louisiana didn't just up and join the Girl Scouts. In fact, black boys and girls weren't allowed to do much of anything at all. Kentwood in the 1960s was a small town split apart by racial tensions. And right there, on three acres smack dab in the middle of the white neighborhood, lived Barbara, her parents, and nine of her eleven brothers and sisters.

Barbara's father, Lawrence Gordon, had no idea what his family was going up against in Kentwood when he made the decision that New Orleans was no place to raise children. He followed his brother-in-law's advice, invested all of his money in the new property and then traversed the seventy-five miles of raised bridges over swamp after swamp to deliver his family to their new home.

No one in the Gordon family could have possibly been prepared for the animosity they faced. Angry neighbors burned crosses on the Gordon's front lawn. Not once, not twice, but over and over again. The first time it happened, seven-year-old

Barbara stood immobilized with fear as she peered out the window at the crosses shooting red flames across her yard. She turned to her father, her protector, and searched for comfort in his face; then she trembled all the more at the emotions she read in his set, grim look. But resistance, the Gordons knew, was out of the question. Black men were lynched for far less. If they wanted to survive, all the family could do was bear up and continue to forge ahead with the many everyday tasks it took to keep the large family fed and warm.

And, after all, not every white family in town was set against the Gordons. One neighbor took pity on the family and gave Lawrence permission to use a few acres of unused land to extend the Gordons' vegetable crops. But other than asking this neighbor for the use of the extra land each year, Lawrence and his family had nothing to do with their white neighbors. In fact, the family was almost completely self-sufficient. They raised chickens and grew their own corn, peanuts, beans, peas, potatoes, tomatoes and watermelons. Barbara's mother, Lillie Mae Gordon, only went to the store for the occasional item to supplement their home-grown goods.

Still and all, for such a large family, funds were tight. Lawrence worked eight hours a day as a janitor at the First Baptist Church, a white church, and then put in another four hours at the post office. With whatever spare time was left, he worked on the family fields. Lillie Mae took in ironing from families in town to try to stay at home with her children as long as she could. But when the Gordons still needed the extra income, she took a job as a maid for a white family. Later she earned her GED and became a teacher's assistant. Barbara's older sister, Brenda, cared for the younger ones while their mother worked during the day. But Lillie Mae was determined to not miss a beat. When she came home from work and her children started tumbling through the door, she demanded an individual report from each child. It took a while: through dinner, through homework, through preparations for bed, Lillie

Mae would not rest until each of her children had detailed his or her activities of the day.

Bedtime in the Gordon's modest, three-bedroom home was an event. Rollaway beds were pulled out into the dining room and living room. Sheets flew up in the air as pull-out couches were transformed into comfy beds. Babies were positioned between bigger children in the double beds that filled the bedrooms. It was noisy. It was hectic. It was busy. But somehow, in the midst of the ruckus, each child would receive a tender goodnight from each parent and a reminder to say his or her prayers.

Barbara was the tenth child. Known as the serious, studious one, Barbara was perhaps the child who suffered the most when the Kentwood schools were integrated. At fourteen, she was one of the black children who filed into their new school only to discover that the white children had been whisked away to a new private school taking with them all the books and most of the school resources. Barbara, nonetheless, flourished in school. A math whiz, she loved to learn, and she quickly became a favorite among the teachers. But at her graduation ceremony, although just a handful of white children remained in the school, the principal would not present Barbara, a black child—a black girl, for God's sake—with the valedictorian plaque. It was not until the next day, when the principal brought the plaque to her house, that it was presented to her parents.

The refusal to publicly acknowledge Barbara's accomplishments hurt. It hurt a lot. She knew she had earned that honor. She had worked so hard. In the end, she tried to shrug it off, saying that it didn't matter; she was leaving Kentwood behind. She was going to college. She would become a doctor and never look back.

～

A mix of grants, loans and part-time work brought Barbara to the University of New Orleans to study pre-med and allowed her to fulfill her mother's wish that she send a little extra money home to her family. But college, she soon realized, was not the dream world she had imagined. Because her family life had been so warm and all-encompassing, she had rarely before had any reason to look outside her extended family for social interaction. Now, out on her own, she couldn't begin to cope with the thousands of confident coeds scurrying purposefully across the campus. She just couldn't see how she, Barbara Gordon, was going to fit into that scene. And as she floundered socially, her studies suffered.

The day Lawrence received Barbara's poor mid-semester grades in the mail, he didn't hesitate. He hopped in the car and drove straight to New Orleans. "Pack your bags," he told his horrified daughter. Barbara certainly did not like disappointing her parents. Worse yet, her competitive spirit screamed in the face of failure. But what choice did she have? She went home.

Mortified to be returning to Kentwood as a college drop-out, Barbara wasted no time enrolling in Southeastern Louisiana University, a local school. She lived at home and took the bus to school. In her very first semester, she made the dean's list and rekindled her relationship with her high school sweetheart. Socially and academically, she was back on track. But it didn't last long. That summer Barbara got the shock of her life: she was pregnant.

For months, Barbara skulked around her house hiding her pregnancy with big shirts. She couldn't stand to think of the disappointment that would show on her parents' faces when they heard the news. She could hardly process it herself. Her mother had so much wanted to see her daughters finish their education and have fulfilling careers. She had warned them again and again not to tie themselves down with kids too early. Barbara felt that she had let her parents down. She had let herself down.

She could only hide her pregnancy so long. The time came to make a decision. Barbara sat down with Gene, her boyfriend of four years, to figure out a plan. They decided that they would do the right thing; they would get married. Without revealing their secret and without wasting another moment of time, the two were wed.

Then, just four days after the wedding, Barbara's father had a massive heart attack right in front of the newlyweds. Barbara cradled her dying father in the back seat of his car as Gene rushed them to the hospital. Ten minutes after their arrival, Lawrence was pronounced dead. Barbara lost it—just lost it. It was all her fault. She was sure he had found out about her pregnancy. His profound disappointment in her must have done him in. From that day on, guilt rode on her back.

A month later, Barbara's mother heard a rumor that her daughter was pregnant. She confronted Barbara, now more than four months along in her pregnancy, with the information. Was it true? Crying, she could only nod her head. Lillie Mae took the news in a matter-of-fact manner. Had she seen a doctor? No? Well, she needed to go right away. Barbara took her mother's advice. For only the third time in her life, the aspiring doctor went to see a doctor.

With new responsibilities on his shoulders, Gene dropped out of his technical school and enlisted in the Air Force. When he came back from basic training, the couple moved to the Air Force base in Biloxi, Mississippi. Knowing that she would have her baby in a strange place, away from her family, broke Barbara's heart all over again. But at least it was a fresh start. And for that, she was ready.

～

Barbara and Gene found a small apartment on the base. Baby Nico, eight pounds, fifteen ounces of pure joy, was born on January 24, 1976 at the base's medical center. Barbara stayed at home with the baby for six months until financial pressures forced her to take a $2.90-an-hour job as a layaway clerk at Wilson's Jewelers and Distributors. Nico went to the daycare center on the base, though she never truly adjusted to being away from her mother. After Barbara cried that she couldn't take another day of hearing her baby girl wail as she kissed her goodbye, Gene took over the task of dropping Nico off at daycare each morning. Barbara, however, was happy to be the one to pick up Nico at the end of the day.

When Nico was three, the family moved to another base, this time in Arizona. Barbara stayed home with her daughter for a year, but when the little girl started kindergarten, she took a job as a long distance telephone operator. Over the years, each time Barbara would call home to Louisiana, her mother could be counted on to ask the same question again and again: When are you going back to school? Barbara didn't have a good answer. She had been asking herself the same question. Her dream of going to medical school was still very much alive. She found herself reading every doctor's biography she could get her hands on. But because Gene was an enlistee, not an officer, money was extremely tight. As they struggled to scrape together the rent on their little studio efficiency, she just didn't see how they could survive without her income.

But as time ticked on, Barbara started to wonder how much longer she could afford to live with herself without getting her degree. In 1980, she threw caution to the wind and enrolled at the Tempe campus of Arizona State University as a part-time, pre-med student. Again, she floundered. Holding down a job, attending school and taking care of a young child didn't leave much time to study for her intense pre-med courses. She dropped out.

Then, in December of 1981, Barbara and Gene split up. Barbara was left with just $500 to find an apartment for herself and Nico. On her own for the first time in her life, she mishandled the money. Expenses she hadn't planned for like the phone, the utilities, and the car payment caught her by surprise. So Barbara and her five-year-old daughter had a place to stay, for a short while, but otherwise they were flat broke.

The wolves were howling at the door. Barbara was absolutely terrified that she and her daughter would wind up homeless or snared in the welfare cycle. Once she fell into the quagmire, how would she pull herself and her child out? What kind of life would that be? What kind of options would she be able to offer her beautiful little girl?

Just when things were at their most desperate, Barbara heard through the National Society of Black Engineers of a position at Bechtel Corporation, one of the largest engineering firms in the world. Always strong in math, she decided to apply. Through affirmative action, she landed the job.

The job was an absolute godsend, but as it was essentially an internship, her salary still wouldn't cover the rent on even the smallest studio apartment, much less other expenses like food and babysitting. With few options, for the next two years, Barbara and Nico rented a room from a string of different families. Barbara hated it, just hated it. It was nerve-racking and oppressive. She always tried to give the family that rented her the room enough space for their own family time. For Barbara and Nico, that meant hiding out in the room they shared and wasting hours wandering through the local mall. Barbara tried renting a room from other single mothers thinking it might make for a more comfortable situation. But she then found herself obsessively worrying that the women would have dangerous men spend the night. She was always fretting about whether her daughter was safe when she wasn't around which sadly was far more of the time than Barbara would have liked.

Barbara essentially sleep-walked through the years following the break-up of her marriage. Her schedule was brutal, especially after she realized she had to have a degree in order to secure her newfound career as an engineer. She re-enrolled in Arizona State in 1983. She attended classes in the morning. Then she picked Nico up from school at 2:15, spent the afternoon driving her to after-school activities, gave Nico dinner and then finally fell into bed for two to three hours of sleep.

At 10:30 at night, she would drag herself out of the house to work the 11:00 to 7:30 graveyard shift at Bechtel.

Once she arrived at work, however, Barbara was on fire. Bechtel had hired her to work on the construction of a nuclear power plant. She worked with a team of engineers to monitor the craftspeople and provide on-site supervision. On January 4, 1982, she walked onto the mammoth construction site for the first time and drew a sharp breath. She knew without doubt she had found her calling. When the engineers took Barbara up to the roof of the turbine deck overlooking the busy construction site, she had to hang onto the railing. She was that dizzy with excitement. The full view of that nuclear power plant under construction was the most awe-inspiring thing she had ever seen or ever could have imagined. The idea of seeing something built. The engineering behind it. The craftsmanship that went into the work. The tools and equipment used to do the work. The problems and the resolution of those problems— every tiny detail was fascinating. For the first time in her life, twenty-four-year-old Barbara knew she had arrived at the right place. "One day," she said to her co-workers, her awe-struck eyes shining bright, "one day I am going to be running this type of project myself."

~

Barbara's plan was to work extremely hard and win the attention of her supervisor. Her plan worked. While her colleagues averaged five percent raises, she received a thirteen percent raise. After two years, she was brought on staff as a permanent employee and was promoted to area field engineer.

The best part of her new job was that even though Barbara's ex-husband had recently cut his child support payments down to the bone, Barbara was at last able to afford rent on an apartment. It wasn't the best apartment and it certainly wasn't in the best part of town. But at least she and her daughter finally had their own space. Barbara hired a woman to spend the night with her daughter while she continued with her brutal schedule. Some weeks she worked seven days a week so that she would be able to put away some money to someday buy a home of her own in a safe neighborhood. She worked so hard she often made herself sick, but as long as she could slowly—oh, so slowly—accumulate college credit hours, she felt that she was moving in the right direction.

At age twenty-seven, Barbara had saved enough money to put a down payment on a townhouse. She couldn't find words to describe the range of emotions she felt the day that her co-workers at Bechtel helped her move her things into a place—a safe place—that finally belonged just to her and her daughter. It was an incredible accomplishment.

But by late 1985, Barbara was seriously burning out. Years of sleep deprivation had taken their toll, and as American sentiment grew against the nuclear power industry, she became apprehensive about the future of her job. Across the nation, nuclear power plants were being designed, but not built. And sure enough, Bechtel did start handing out pink slips.

Barbara couldn't afford to wait for the axe to fall. Though she hated to leave her new townhouse and drop out of college yet again, she remembered all too clearly the sound of those wolves at her door. Her finances were too tight to be out of work for any amount of time, so she accepted a job at a nuclear power plant in Oswego, a small town in upstate New York.

Oswego was a far cry from Arizona. It was cold, brutally cold, in more ways than one. As the only black girl in the fourth grade class of her school, Nico daily faced an onslaught of name-calling and teasing. Only one little girl in the entire school was willing to call her friend. Barbara had had no clue that Oswego would be so culturally monochromatic. It tore her apart to see her child exposed to the same racist slander she had faced so many years ago in Louisiana. Although she loved her job, she soon began searching for another one.

After working just nine months in New York, she found a job as an engineer at a nuclear plant in Texas. Sadly for Barbara, the job was not in construction. Nuclear plants simply weren't being built anymore, so Barbara took what she could find: a position as an environmental qualification engineer. Her job was to do fault and failure analysis to determine if a part made of organic materials, a rubber seal, for example, would operate were an accident to occur.

After three months, the company transferred her to Nebraska. On Christmas Eve of that same year, 1987, she was laid off. Barbara got in touch with her old boss in Texas and nearly cried in relief when she learned her old job was still waiting for her. A year later, however, her project ended and she was again unemployed and terrified of winding up on the dole. She quickly found a consulting job in Connecticut and once again she and Nico relocated across the country.

Though Barbara had little choice but to go where she could find work, her heart broke each time she had to pack her bags. There were too many first days of school for her young daughter—just too many. And Barbara herself struggled to squeeze in a class or two at a university at every stop along the way. She feared she would never enjoy any measure of security until she at last had her degree. Always, she felt like she was just one step away from losing the small gains she had made. The wolves never quieted at her door.

≈

In Connecticut, Barbara's odyssey back and forth across the country finally came to a halt. She met and married Fritz Armand. The day after the wedding, the two set down roots and bought a house in New Jersey. Barbara's new husband, an engineer himself, wanted to kick off the marriage by starting a business together. He argued: Why work for someone else? Where has that gotten us so far? Barbara had never considered starting a business before. But she was already working in Connecticut as a consultant, so the idea wasn't much of a stretch to her. The two tossed around ideas for starting a variety of businesses, but the one thing Barbara kept going back to was that they should stick with what they knew. They decided to start a professional services firm focused on construction management and engineering.

On April 16, 1991, Barbara's thirty-fifth birthday, Armand Corporation was officially incorporated. Chills ran up and down Barbara's spine when she received the articles of incorporation in the mail. She could see her future laid out in front of her, and she liked what she saw. They would create a business, an institution really, with nice offices, nice employees and nice clients—an organization that would last until the day they decided to sell the business and retire off the proceeds. It would bring Barbara the financial security that had always eluded her.

Barbara had only one accounting course and one business law course under her belt and Fritz had zero business experience. Neither of them had ever held a management position. Despite their inexperience, Barbara was completely confident that the business would succeed. Somehow.

With $2,000 from an income tax refund and a few credit cards to work with as startup money, Barbara began working full time on the business while Fritz held a job to support the household. After converting an upstairs bedroom of their home into an office, she took a deep breath, picked up the phone and started dialing.

With practice, the cold calling got easier. Then Barbara was invited to her first meeting. She walked into a room full of white men and her knees almost gave out beneath her. She survived that first meeting but quaked to think of ever again facing a second. Her husband encouraged her to keep trying. "You are as good as they are," he told her. "You belong there. You know your stuff."

Barbara nodded as her husband tried to buoy her confidence even as she trembled at the thought of again presenting her skills in front of a room full of white men. Then she met Hanford Jones, an advocate with the City of Philadelphia Minority Business Enterprise Council. Hanford was a jewel among men. An African American himself, he made finding new business for Armand Corporation his personal mission. When Barbara confided her intimidation at attending meetings where she was the only African American *and* the only woman, he said, "No problem, I will go with you."

Barbara took Hanford up on his offer a few times until it struck her that as long as she entered the meeting room with a smile and a confident attitude, the men were more than happy to talk business. Still, Hanford remained a solid force behind Barbara, encouraging her to aggressively go after new business. His encouragement paid off. Armand Corporation was awarded its first contract: a demolition deal no other construction management company would touch.

Philadelphia's old JFK Stadium had historical significance, but it had to come down. It was old, so old that the original drawings for the stadium couldn't even be found. Developing a demolition procedure for a stadium with no drawings was risky business. Barbara hired a structural engineer and developed the plan. On the day of the demolition, Barbara held her breath as section after section of the stadium was demolished exactly according to her plan. There was not a single mishap. With wide eyes, she watched the stadium fall bleacher by bleacher, bit by bit, overwhelmed by the sensation that everything in her life had led her to just that project at just that point in time. She had pulled it off. Armand Corporation was officially launched.

∾

The job paid $23,000, and the money couldn't have come along at a better time. The Armands had failed to recognize the full extent of the economic recession the country was undergoing. There simply was little work to be had in construction in the early 1990s.

But with that first job, Armand Corporation started to carve out a niche for itself as a firm that wasn't afraid to take risks. Still, times were tight. And money got tighter yet when, in 1993, Fritz was laid off from his job. He began working full-time with Armand Corporation, now housed in the Armand's garage. He took the job of executive vice president. Barbara served as president and also held responsibilities as the CEO, CFO, COO and the janitor. Though uneasy about losing the income, Barbara was optimistic the company would come along faster with more than one person working on it.

Barbara's hopes were further ignited that year because, although the business was struggling each and every day, another miracle was in the making. Fritz had run into their house one day yelling about an unusual college he had heard about on the radio. The Thomas Edison State College evaluated college credit hours for people who had fallen short on finishing their degrees and awarded a degree to those who finished the necessary credit hours at any local university. Barbara's eyes lit up and she ran to her closet to fetch a shoebox overflowing with transcripts from all the universities she had attended across the country. After the college had evaluated her credits, an astonished Barbara learned that she needed only nine credit hours to finish.

Straight away, she enrolled in three humanities courses at Rutgers, the same college Nico was attending. Barbara bought a cell phone and explained to her professors that she was running a business and might need to step away on occasion to take an important call. They understood. After completing her classes and passing an oral exam in physics, Barbara was awarded a degree in mathematics and natural sciences with a concentration in physics. It had taken her a total of nineteen years from the day she took her first class at the University of

New Orleans. She didn't care. She had done it. Nothing could stop her now.

But her troubles were far from over. Shortly after Fritz joined the company, Armand Corporation won a construction management project on a coal fire plant in Indonesia. Fritz went to Indonesia to oversee the project while Barbara worked on a few small contracts back home. After four months, Fritz's project ended and he came back to New Jersey to help his wife face a dire financial situation. Barbara had approached a number of financial institutions for financing, but without adequate collateral, bank after bank turned her down. After she paid Nico's college tuition, there was simply nothing left to cover household expenses. Her Toyota Corolla was repossessed and the mortgage company threatened to foreclose on the house. The situation was desperate.

The Armands managed to hold off the mortgage company, but in early 1994, Fritz's SUV was repossessed, leaving the Armands without a car. Over the few weeks it took to scrape together the money to spring the SUV, the Armands borrowed a car for business meetings from a young man willing to work for their company for "the experience" at little to no salary. Once, Barbara found herself stranded with his car in a parking garage without even the five dollars needed to get out of the lot. Luckily, she secured a loan from the driver in the car behind her who happened to be an acquaintance.

Meanwhile, she fell behind on her daughter's tuition payments and Nico was deregistered. Barbara told her daughter to keep going to classes. She would somehow find a way to keep her in school. Barbara took the next day off of work to go to Rutgers and beg the financial aid office to help her daughter. She so desperately wanted Nico to stay in school. A financial aid officer took pity on the overwrought mother and scraped together $2,100 in grants and scholarships. Well, that solved one problem, but the Armands and their business were still in dire financial straits. Stress levels in the household hit a new high and Fritz decided to start looking for a job. Then, just as he started to send out his resume, the economy turned the corner and Armand Corporation suddenly won several significant new contracts. They had done it. They had actually pulled through.

By the end of 1994, Armand Corporation was flying high. The company moved out of the garage and into a beautiful new office. Fritz started up a new construction division so that, in addition to offering professional services, Armand Corporation could handle the actual heavy lifting. Meanwhile the other divisions, construction management and engineering, were taking off. In 1995, the Armands hired fifteen new employees. Revenues climbed from $200,000 in 1993; to $800,000 in 1994; to $2,000,000 in 1995.

The wolves at her door had finally quieted. For Barbara, it was the sweetest silence. The sense of relief was indescribable. Barbara was enjoying financial security for the first time in her life. The arrival of a bill in the mail no longer sent her flying into a panic. She could walk into a store without having to mentally count the pennies in her pocket. The Armands even began developing plans to build their dream home. They had made it.

~

By 1997, Armand Corporation had over sixty employees and annual revenue in the $5 million range. The company had won contract after contract in industries such as transportation, utilities, commercial buildings, housing and institutional facilities. Armand Corporation maintained their reputation as the firm that would go anywhere, do anything and get the job done right. Barbara accepted contracts, for example, for public housing projects that no one else wanted to touch. The company picked up techniques for minimizing risks.

Whenever they worked in a bad neighborhood, they got their schedule down to a science. They learned when it was a safe time to be in a neighborhood and when you just had to get out.

At the same time, Barbara, unhappily enough, was learning a personal lesson about getting out at the right time. Though Armand Corporation was thriving, the Armand household was imploding. In August of 1997, just a few months after they had moved into their new home, Barbara and Fritz called their relationship quits. They tried to work together in the business for a few months, but the tensions proved insurmountable. They finally recognized that they couldn't maintain a professional environment while going through a separation. So Fritz left the company.

It was a painful, complicated divorce. The Armands not only had to split the financial assets of the household; there was the business to contend with. While the divorce proceedings took place, stretching from February 1998 through August 1999, the judge froze the Armand's assets. Barbara was told that she could not sell any corporate assets, refinance the company debt or raise capital. As these restraints slowly but surely began to sink the company, she decided to close down the construction division that Fritz had managed, the least profitable and most resource-intensive division of Armand Corporation. For the sake of her own integrity, she had the crews finish up every job they had started, even as Armand Corporation bled money with each passing day. When each project ended, the layoffs began.

Closing the division did not cut deeply enough. By the time she had regained financial control over her business and pulled together the funds to buy out her ex-husband's share of the business, the company was down to only twenty employees and Barbara herself was hovering on the brink of personal bankruptcy.

Again, the wolves howled at the door. Barbara had enjoyed only three years of financial stability. She knew all too well how to scrimp and save and hold off creditors; but she was anguished by the sense that she had gone backwards. Backtracking hurt. Her parents had a phrase: "Easy does it; steady, but forward." She knew there was only one way out of her plight— forward march. She prayed for the strength to help her rebuild her business and her life.

Barbara received a substantial boost when a New Jersey bank, Gloucester County Federal Savings Bank, refinanced her company's debt and gave her the first line of credit she had ever had. It allowed her to pay off some debt and start pulling her company out of its financial mire. More than that, the loan officers saw through the financial mess her business had become. They saw Barbara, and they believed in her. They gave her a chance, and she ran with it.

Barbara quickly realized that the road to rebuilding Armand Corporation was not just about winning more business. She had to make Armand Corporation a better company. That meant stepping up the quality of its services, its people, its projects. Only then could Armand Corporation compete at a higher level.

First, Barbara started a technology division to address the communications problems she saw rise up on so many construction projects. Good communications systems ensured that mistakes would not happen and that projects would not flounder. A concrete result of this new division's worth was an increase in the number of large projects awarded to Armand Corporation. For example, the company was selected as a systems integrator for a huge construction project for JFK Airport in New York. Armand Corporation provided the communications network system solutions for the flight information display, gate management, common use terminal equipment, baggage reconciliation, airport operational database and integrated network management.

And as Armand Corporation expanded its services and its reputation for excellence, a diverse roster of big-name clients came on board including American Airlines, Sprint, the U.S. Army, the U.S. Navy, Marriott Corporation and Johnson & Johnson. Barbara has also been successful cultivating another crucial aspect for her business—profitability. In 2002, with thirty-eight employees, Armand had revenues of $2.7 million. In 2003, she anticipates growth of more than fifty percent.

It didn't happen with just the snap of her fingers. Getting back on track was no easy task. And Barbara still works far more hours than she would like. She spends most of her day in her office troubleshooting problem after problem that crosses her desk.

But it's the interruptions from the daily grind that make it all so worthwhile. Her daughter, now a graduate student studying creative writing at Johns Hopkins University, calls her on almost a daily basis. And Barbara really enjoys getting out of her office to meet with clients. She smiles now to think back on the days when she would walk into a conference room with her knees knocking. She no longer minds standing out as the only African American woman in the room. In fact, she sort of likes it. She is proud of who she has become and what she has accomplished.

Barbara gets tremendous satisfaction when she walks through her office building and sees the ethnically diverse faces of the civil engineers, the surveyors, the electrical and mechanical engineers, the construction managers, the estimators and the inspectors: the people who make Armand Corporation what it is today. She relishes watching them doing well, buying homes, taking vacations, putting their kids through college— much of it due to the financial security they are able to draw from Armand Corporation.

Against the odds, Barbara has managed to keep the wolves at bay for herself, for her company and for her employees. Peace and complacency, however, are not one in the same. She is constantly trying to work out how she can make Armand Corporation bigger and better. She dreams of someday acquiring other businesses so that Armand Corporation will have offices around the country. Big dreams, no doubt, but Barbara has already seen so many miracles in her lifetime. She knows that anything is possible.

KEEPING IT ═══════
IN THE FAMILY

VAN EURE ═══════
CEO and Owner, The Angus Barn
Raleigh, North Carolina

S HE OWNS a sprawling world-renowned restaurant, but shares a small windowless office with an employee of eighteen years. She is an animal rights activist, but makes her living serving juicy steaks. She has traveled the world, but is happiest working side by side with the employees she has known for over forty years.

She could do anything, be anywhere, have *everything*, but works until 2:00 A.M. on weekdays, Saturdays, Sundays and holidays serving others.

Van Eure has hiked Mt. Kilimanjaro, started a Montessori school in Kenya, won international wine awards and calls Ken Blanchard a dear friend. She comes to work in slip-resistant athletic shoes, hands out "good luck" apples to departing customers and focuses a good deal of time on how to turn around unhappy diners so that every single visitor leaves full and happy. And all the while, she never stops planning, never stops dreaming, never stops working to make the Angus Barn the best restaurant in the world for customers and employees alike.

With 240 employees and annual sales of over $10 million, Van's 650-seat restaurant is one of the most successful in the country. Ranked consistently near the top by every national trade publication, the Angus Barn serves more than a quarter of a million steaks a year. Then there are lobster tails and shrimp. Prime rib and leg of lamb. And don't forget your blackberry cobbler or a slice of Van's mother's Chocolate Chess Pie.

~

It all started back in 1959. Five-year-old Van had a father with a dream: to open a country restaurant that would display the farm implements and antique junk he had collected. Along with a college buddy, he bought five acres of land in the middle of nowhere, just outside the city of Raleigh, North Carolina.

Finding the money to construct a 275-seat restaurant posed the first big challenge. The partners borrowed what they could from anyone willing to fork over cash. Then Van's legendary grandfather, Thad Eure, Sr., who served for fifty-two years as North Carolina's secretary of state, took a risk on the two hopefuls and put up his home to guarantee their loan. One thing was sure: Thad must have really loved his son. Restaurateurs these two were not. They were just men with growing families and routine jobs who decided a decent steakhouse was exactly what their hometown needed.

Van's mother, on the other hand, wasn't so sure about her husband's plans. When he laid out his vision to her, she cried for three solid days. What did her husband know about the restaurant business? He couldn't even cook! He would lose everything they had built. Then she did what she had always done in a marriage she regarded as a true partnership: she joined her husband by his side. In fact, it was her sense of style and eye for design that made the Angus Barn what it is today—a huge red barn that feels like home.

Somehow, against the odds, the partners seemed to make all the right decisions. The location, the atmosphere, the cuisine, the approach, everything clicked. They were on their way.

Van's parents spent most of their time at the restaurant. They planned the menus, put up decorations, ran the cash register, seated customers and, if need be, they washed dishes and cleaned the bathrooms.

Van and her brother and sister virtually grew up in the Barn. As the restaurant took off and thrived, the Eures went from

44

penny pinching to being in a position to give their three children everything their hearts could desire. This, the Eures realized, could be a problem. So they laid down the law: no allowances, no convertibles wrapped in big bows to be found sitting in the driveway, no easy ride. The kids would work to earn the things they wanted. At age fifteen, Van took a waitressing job at the Angus Barn to save money to buy her first car.

Van became incredibly independent for a girl her age, and with that independence came rebellion. Much of the target of that rebellion was the man with the stubborn, determined personality so similar to her own—her father. Father and daughter clashed for many years. So when Van graduated from the University of North Carolina, although she had no idea what she *would* do, she knew what she *wouldn't* do. She wanted to get as far away from her father and "his" restaurant as possible.

Many of her friends were going to Europe, but that seemed too obvious, too common, too tame. Anyone could do that. No, Van craved a radical adventure. She spun her globe and decided to travel to the other side of the world. She would visit a third world country. Bold and brash, twenty-three-year-old Van set off for Kenya. An athlete and a competitor, she embarked on a three-month mountain climbing program organized by the National Outdoor Leadership School.

The moment she stepped off the plane in Kenya, Van was overwhelmed by a sense of belonging. This was it. She had found her place. She connected with the people, the lifestyle and the natural terrain in a way she couldn't even begin to define. It was almost as if she had lived there in another lifetime. She savored the deep respect the culture commanded toward elders and teachers. She was moved by how content and happy the people were despite having almost no material possessions. In the midst of a melting pot of differences, there was a society of tolerance. Some women covered up every part of their body except their eyes. Other women openly nursed their babies on the bus. Everyone was accepted. For Van, this just felt right.

The three-month program flew by and Van felt that she had just begun to taste this new world. The morning of her scheduled departure, she demurely traveled with her group to the airport. But when the moment came to board the plane, she just couldn't do it. She wasn't ready to say goodbye to her new life. She watched the plane take off without her. Then she slung her bag over her shoulder and walked out of the airport.

Worried about her parent's response, Van didn't break the news until she had landed a job teaching swimming and English. Then she told them that she wasn't coming home. Her parents were not surprised. They knew their daughter's nature and were relieved that she had finally found something that spoke to her.

As she tuned into the culture, Van employed her passion for helping others by starting a Montessori school. She loved the Montessori concept of letting the children, young and old, learn from each other. Van had found a way that she could make a difference. She taught for five years, falling more and more in love with the country and the people.

During her years in Kenya, Van escaped from the panty hose, alarm clocks and over-processed food of American society. She wore reasonable, comfortable clothing. She woke with the sunlight. She learned how to cook in a pit. She had a sense that, for the first time, she was experiencing a real life.

As it had before, her don't-tell-me-I-can't-do-it attitude energized her and she was always on the prowl for something to prove. Climbing expeditions on both Mount Kilimanjaro and Mount Kenya brought Van face-to-face with some of the most challenging feats of her life. She spent three weeks on Mount Kenya in the coldest conditions she had ever experienced. But day after day, she pushed on, step by step, blinded by relentless driving snow. One evening, she struggled to set up her tent in a high wind, then finally crawled inside. With feet so frozen that she expected her toes to break off, exhausted and almost unable to breathe, she rolled into her sleeping bag. Lying there, awake in the total darkness, she asked herself the pointed question: Van, what the hell are you doing here?

But she knew why she was there. She was finding herself, finding the person that she knew she could become. With everything she had been given in life, she knew that more than having an opportunity to do something great, she had an obligation to do something great. How *dare* she not make a difference?

~

The quest for greatness, however, was temporarily thrust aside when Van fell in love with a man from Australia. When a marriage proposal followed, twenty-seven-year-old Van had an enthusiastic "yes" on the ready. Then, en route to Australia, she brought her fiancé home to meet her family. Van closely watched the way her fiancé treated her family and found she saw something new in the man. Something she couldn't quite put a finger on. Something she didn't like. Suddenly, she knew without doubt that he was not the right man for her. Once again, she watched a plane take off without her. She stayed in Raleigh and took a job bartending at Darryl's, another restaurant her father had started.

Now back in her hometown, Van had no idea that she would miss Kenya so passionately. She pined for the country—the open plains, the animals, the people, the climate. She spent her days teaching aerobics and dreaming about a life that no longer existed. She spent her nights bartending. All the while she was trying to figure out what to do with her life.

Although she'd promised herself she would never again work at the Angus Barn, she found it was the easiest way to pull herself back into the world. Her father was just opening a new bar at the restaurant called the Wild Turkey Lounge, and she decided she'd work with him "for awhile."

That first step was the beginning of years of mentoring by her father. During those years they began to talk, really talk. They learned to see each other in a different light. And they learned to laugh together, realizing they shared the same wicked sense of humor. For the first time, they developed a true father-daughter relationship, a blessing in both their lives.

While she had been in Kenya, Van's brother and sister had moved on, deliberately choosing lives far removed from the restaurant. Van had wanted to steer clear of the responsibility as well. But then one day in 1988, six years after she had started working with her father, he sat her down to talk about the future. He told her that he would like to think that the Barn would go on for a long, long time. That it was important to him that the restaurant, his legacy, would remain in the family.

Van didn't know what to say. This was not the life she had planned, but her years in Kenya had taught her to value family and tradition. The thought of losing the family restaurant pained her. She imagined driving past the big red barn knowing that she had never even tried to keep it in the family. She turned to her father, the man she had once sworn to never work with, and said, "I'm still not sure, but I want to try."

A few months later, Van's father was diagnosed with an aggressive form of cancer. As Van saw her father wasting away in the last days of his life, she sat down and wrote a ten-page letter pouring out all she had learned from him, and promising that she would continue to nurture and grow the legacy he had left her, his beloved "Big Red."

At fifty-six years of age, Van's father died in November of 1988, after a three-month battle with pancreatic cancer. While growing his restaurant from 275 to 650 seats, he had made his name as one of the most respected figures in the restaurant world. Among other honors, he had served as president of the National Restaurant Association and his name and reputation were legendary. Those in the industry also knew Van's reputation; they had heard tales of her wild and impetuous life. So, when Van's father died, industry experts and locals alike predicted that the Angus Barn would either be sold or go downhill fast.

Back in those days, the restaurant business was considered a man's world, and the talk was that a woman couldn't run a restaurant that large. "Oh, sure, a woman can run a diner or a little coffee shop," they said, "but a 650-seat restaurant like the Angus Barn, that's a man's job." Hearing comments like this kicked Van into overdrive. She made up her mind to work day and night, seven days a week. She would show them. Not only would she maintain the restaurant, she would make it world famous.

∾

But first some things had to change. For one, Van's years in Kenya, a place where wildlife largely runs free, made her sensitive to the treatment of animals. There wouldn't be any milk-fed veal on the Angus Barn menu. Van made sure that she didn't buy meat from any sources that didn't raise and slaughter animals humanely.

Second, Van knew she couldn't just step into her father's shoes. She needed to find a management style that suited her and allowed her to capitalize on the people who had been the lifeblood of the restaurant from day one. She recognized that many of the employees were far more experienced than she was. These were employees who had adored her since her childhood: people like Betty Shugart, who had been a part of the team for thirty-eight years and Earl Barnes who had been there twenty-five years.

Over the next several months, Van invested in seminars and books, searching for a management approach that she could replicate. It was two years later, at the Monterey Wine Festival that she first heard Ken Blanchard speak. She nodded in agreement with every statement he made. His management philosophy exactly reflected the way she wanted to run the Angus Barn. She wanted to create an environment where all of the employees would be empowered to have a huge say in how things were done.

Following that seminar, Van bought everything with Ken's name on it. She read all his books and listened to all his tapes. She was so onboard with his management approach that she wanted to share it with all of her employees, and decided that the best way to do that was to host him as a speaker.

But the only way she could cover his hefty fee was to hold a public seminar at the restaurant. She sat down and wrote a personal letter to Ken explaining how excited she would be to host him and how she could fill the house. A few days later, the phone rang and Van was startled to hear Ken Blanchard, himself, saying, "Yes, of course," he'd love to come to the Angus Barn.

Not only did Ken come to her restaurant to present that very successful seminar, but ten years later, he and Van are still the best of friends. Every time he comes out her way, he stops by for a meal. He even celebrated his sixty-fifth birthday at the Angus Barn. And Van doesn't think twice about picking up the phone and calling him for advice.

In true Ken Blanchard style, Van seeks continuous input and action from all levels of her staff. Angus Barn employees understand that it is their responsibility to ensure that every customer leaves totally satisfied. And they are empowered to do whatever it takes to make that happen. Van's mantra is: "See it. Own it. Solve it. Do it." A waiter can choose to comp a meal or provide a free dessert if a customer is unhappy. A waitress, ready to take a plate out, is expected to tell the cook if the presentation is not just right. A hostess can suggest a radically different way to accept reservations.

The Angus Barn team refers to this ownership approach as the "Twenty-Foot Rule." Whenever an issue arises, the solution is expected to come from within twenty feet of the problem. In most restaurants, a problem on the cooking line is passed up to someone in ivory tower management. Van believes that the solution to a problem on the cooking line lies within twenty feet of that area. So she doesn't try to solve it with managers and people who are not physically doing the job. Instead she asks the cooks, "How can we solve this problem?" Nine times out of ten, they know the answer.

∾

The "executive office suite" at the Angus Barn is another indicator of Van's progressive management style. She has preserved her father's original office, a nine-by-twelve-foot space smaller than most executives' closets. "In a restaurant," her father used to say, "no money is being made in the office." And Van walks that talk. She shares a windowless office, and in fact a desk, with her long-time assistant, Jill Highsmith. Here she has carried on her father's tradition of "wallpapering" the office with pictures of employees and their children, customers and their cars, friends and their dogs, and neighbors and their grandchildren. While most business owners consider a corner office with a window an absolute necessity, Van prefers to glance up and see smiling employees, customers, and friends.

Van spends as little time as possible in the office and as much time as possible with her customers. This attitude is adopted by her staff as well. In our pass-the-food-through-the-window society, there is a startling difference between a hostess who takes time to chat with you when you come in the door, and one who mumbles the standard "smoking or non-smoking" refrain that has become the typical greeting in most restaurants. There is something about having a server who is more preoccupied with remembering your name than with telling you his. Van has learned that people just want to feel special and small personal touches go a long way.

This focus on the customers rather than the trappings of the business is the hallmark of Van's management style. And she has learned that hiring the right employees is the foundation of customer satisfaction. Often in the restaurant industry, if a waiter can carry a plate and fill a glass, he's hired. Traditions like that drive the industry's average turnover rate of seventy-four percent, a key factor in both the low profitability and the poor customer service that plague many restaurants. But, at the Angus Barn, where the turnover rate is fourteen percent, things are vastly different. It is not uncommon for Angus Barn management to interview 100 applicants to fill two positions. From dishwasher to office staff to head chef, each applicant faces elaborate reference checks and a series of interviews. Then, before a job offer is made, everyone involved in the decision must give a unanimous thumbs up. A safecracker could break into Fort Knox more easily than a mediocre employee could get on the Angus Barn payroll. As a result, all 240 employees wear their Angus Barn employment as a badge of honor. And, once they make it in, they guard the door to ensure that the next employee meets the same high standards.

But it wasn't always that way. Early on, Van wasted time and energy hiring and training employees that she thought she could "save." Finally she learned that good employees can't be made. Oh, sure, you can train for skills, but you can't train for attitude. Understandably, her reliance on a large staff as the lifeblood of her business has caused her considerable stress. From time to time, she has actually wanted to throw in the towel because of that stress. But, over the years, what has hurt the most are experiences of betrayal by the very employees that she works so hard to support.

Her discovery, a few years back, of a drug problem among key staff was a particularly painful episode. Although she sensed that something was wrong, she couldn't admit it, even to herself. Finally she was forced to take decisive action and brought in an undercover agent as a member of the kitchen staff. He quickly learned that the parking lot of the Angus Barn was a meeting point for the exchange of drugs. Just like in the movies, they set up a sting operation which resulted in the arrest of six cooks and several other employees. The experience shocked loyal employees and threatened to tarnish the reputation of the restaurant. Van felt betrayed. How could the very individuals she had trusted, deceive her? The experience took a real toll on her and taught her that she didn't need to "save" people. She can only do what is in her power to do—offer a great place to work and consistently maintain a high caliber of employee.

∾

Each night those employees are put to the test. With an average of 900 customers a night and all the variables that go along with each order—Diet Pepsi, no ice; house salad, dressing on the side; prime rib, medium rare; side order of asparagus, but no hollandaise; twice baked potato, on second thought, make it fries; pie á la mode, but can you let me have that ice cream on the side instead of on top—it's just a matter of time before a slipup occurs. And, when the inevitable happens, Van has developed an ingenious method to soothe ruffled feathers. Think of it as "Lights, Cameras, Action."

Whenever customers get so upset that even the staff's ability to comp a meal or offer a free dessert doesn't placate them, Van steps in to play a game that she has devised. In her game, she is on a movie set. The customer plays the role of an angry customer and Van casts herself as the restaurant owner whose job it is to win back the goodwill of the customer.

Out of the corner of her eye, she "sees" the director as he says, "Okay, let's role. Take one." Van slides into character and works to turn the customer around. Thinking this way, even when a customer is in her face, she's able to maintain her calm and focus on her role as the peacemaking restaurant owner. This approach allows her to remove her personal feelings from the scene, and handle the situation very logically. She has gotten so good at this role playing that sometimes when she approaches a situation, she will size it up and challenge herself by saying, "Hmmm, I bet I can turn this guy around in less than three minutes." Sure enough, by the time she has finished the customer is apologizing to *her*.

Delivering a medium when a medium rare was ordered is bad enough, but the kind of slipups that Van hates the most are those involving special occasions like somebody's birthday or a graduation party. Her approach in these situations is never to ask, "What do you want me to do for you?" but rather to say, "Let me tell you what I'm going to do." Then she always does more than she promises. Van's customer service philosophy is simple—there is no request too great from a customer. As long as it is not illegal, immoral, or unethical, it will be granted.

The morning after a less-than-perfect twenty-first birthday party, Van sent flowers to the home of the honoree. The mother, who had set up the dinner and been very upset by the mix-up, ultimately called to tell the banquet manager how wonderful everything was and how excited her daughter was to receive flowers from the Angus Barn. Van has learned that accidents occur; things go wrong and the unexpected can happen. The key is to remember that no matter how heated a situation may become, what really counts is the final outcome.

A perfect example of this was when the television show, "48-Hours," did a piece on "The Decline of Customer Service in America." They searched the entire country to find a place where service is still alive and well and the Angus Barn was chosen to be put to the test. One evening a "48-Hours" reporter posing as a "customer from hell" visited the restaurant. Wearing a secret wire, the woman was difficult from the word go.

She complained about the table, the noise, the wine and every course that she was served. Although the staff provided immediate solutions, the customer persisted. At the end of the meal, Van walked over to step into her role. Approaching the table she thought, "This is going to be a tough one," only to discover that the reporter had in fact been wildly satisfied with the solutions to the issues raised during the meal. The Angus Barn was singled out on national television as the one restaurant where customer service still reigned.

The Angus Barn might also well be the only "barn" in America that can boast a 30,000-bottle wine cellar. When Van first waited tables as a teenager, the Angus Barn offered only three wines: red, white or rose. Then, on one of his many trips to the West Coast, her father developed an avid interest in wine and decided that the Angus Barn would have a wine list equal to the restaurants in California. Local businesspeople told him he was crazy. "North Carolina is a redneck state," they said. "People here just want their beer and bourbon." But there was no stopping him when he was set on a mission.

From the initial offering of three wines, the list grew, until eventually they required a small wine cellar for their 300 bottles. The selection continued to expand, outgrowing the initial cellar and creeping into every nook and cranny of the restaurant. The next step, and it was a daring one for a restaurant in the Bible Belt state of North Carolina, was to place an Angus Barn-labeled wine bottle on every table. This risky decision ultimately caused customers to consider wine a critical component of an Angus Barn experience. As a result, the wine list continued to grow and grow like the kudzu that is so familiar in the Angus Barn's part of the country.

When Van took over, she got the notion to research international wine awards and discovered the prestigious *Wine Spectator* Grande Award which has very strict requirements.

To qualify, a restaurant's wine list must represent every major wine producing country and region in the world. To ensure the availability of each wine on the list, a stringent formula must be followed. Because the Angus Barn seats 650, they are required to stock thirty cases of each of the 1,350 wines included on their list. Moving up to this level was a major strategic and financial decision for the restaurant, but they decided to go for it.

Again, the risk paid off. Although they didn't win the award on their first submission, they continued to apply and received the award on their third try. In 1989, four restaurants in the world won the Grande Award. One was in France, one was in Switzerland, one was in California and one was in Raleigh, North Carolina.

Excited and bursting with pride, Van and her mother traveled to New York to receive the award. During the evening people asked her again and again, "Now where exactly in Europe is Raleigh?" or "What part of California is Raleigh located in?" And every time someone would ask, Van would break into a wide smile and respond in her thick southern accent that Raleigh was in the great state of North Carolina. In the world of wine, the Angus Barn had put Van's home state on the map.

As a result of winning the award, guests began asking, "Can we see your wine cellar?" Well, the Angus Barn still had wine stuffed here and there. They had a grungy basement where they stored their extra cases, but it wasn't at all what could be called a wine cellar. As Van led guests down a flight of rickety stairs into the dark basement, she would hold her breath praying that they wouldn't trip and fall. When they reached the bottom, guests would try to disguise their disappointment. There really wasn't much to see; just cases of wine locked in cages—not at all what they expected of the award-winning Angus Barn Wine Cellar.

After suffering this embarrassment for a few months, Van began planning to build a wine cellar equal to the award. As the plans evolved, she decided to add a special gourmet dining room just off of the wine cellar. Because the Angus Barn had always been a meat-and-potatoes kind of place, neither Van nor her staff knew anything about gourmet cooking. So she hired two French chefs to come in and teach a crash course on the basics. The Angus Barn's chefs came out of the training with a repertoire of four appetizers, four salads, four entrees and four desserts. This was enough to get them started when the Wine Cellar Dining Room opened.

As the dining room reached completion, Van realized that this area would require special service. The traditional red and white gingham, so appropriate in the "down home" atmosphere of the general dining area, gave way to the tuxedos and white gloves demanded by the wine cellar's exquisitely furnished dining room. Finally, Van brought on a Cellar Master to announce and explain the courses and corresponding wines to those guests lucky enough to experience a Wine Cellar meal. One of these meals is truly something to write home about. Corporate executives often reserve the room for out-of-town clients and there is no place more impressive to close a big deal than in the richly-paneled room.

As proof that the wine cellar and the Wine Cellar Dining Room were not part of the original restaurant plans, guests must pass through the kitchen to reach them. But the staff uses what could be considered an intrusion as yet another opportunity to shine. From head chef to dishwasher, each employee stops whatever he is doing to smile and greet guests as they pass through the kitchen. As the parade of men in their business suits and women in their finery rounds the corner into the kitchen, a member of the staff is sure to approach the guests with a "We're so glad to see you at the Angus Barn."

∿

Running an establishment like the Angus Barn is a full-time job and then some. And although Van seems to have the whole life-balance thing under control, it wasn't always this way. As she celebrated her fortieth birthday, Van was married to the Angus Barn. Working for weeks on end without taking a day off and with a non-existent social life, she assumed the restaurant would be the only spouse she would ever have. Then Steve Thanhauser, an advertising executive, stepped into her life.

A divorced, single parent, Steve asked Van out five times. Five times she shot him down. How could a nice guy like Steve possibly find a place in her hectic life? But Steve proved as stubborn as Van. Finally, she agreed to meet him at the movies. And she agreed to the next date. And the next. And the next.

In June 1997, she exchanged vows with Steve in a wedding held in her mother's back yard. The joy was short lived. A mere three months later, Van's mother died of cancer. More than just losing her beloved mother, Van was left with the restaurant to manage on her own in addition to settling in with a new husband and stepchild. Getting married was a startling revelation. Van was used to being on her own. Both she and Steve had to make major adjustments to make their marriage work. But Steve proved to be a great stabilizing force in Van's life and was there to help with whatever she needed, offering his calm and quiet support.

In the beginning of her marriage, Van worked eighty or ninety hours a week, trying to hold the Barn to the standards her parents would have wanted. At the same time, something strange was happening to her. She just didn't feel good. Her body was changing. She assumed the worst: cancer. The reality was a shock of an entirely different nature. At forty-two, Van discovered she had just made it through her first trimester of pregnancy.

It seemed impossible to take it in: How would an infant fit into their already hectic lives? The news put Van on a rollercoaster ride of emotions. One minute she was weeping tears of joy at the thought of bringing her little one home. The next she was despairing that she couldn't possibly manage her expanding family and business without her mother at her side. She tried to bury her emotions in her job. She worked straight up to the day she delivered baby "Ali," short for Alice, named after her mother.

After much trial and error, Van finally figured out how to maintain her breakneck pace at work, keep her family happy and still have time for herself. The secret to her success is maintaining a solid routine. Van works five nights a week, including weekends. However, without fail, she reserves Tuesday night for family night and Thursday night for date night. A typical work night brings her home at two or three in the morning. Before going to bed, she makes sure to set her alarm so that she can get up early enough to spend one-on-one time with her stepson, Christopher, before he leaves for school. Then she heads back to bed to catch a few more hours of sleep before waking again to concentrate on her daughter.

Van made another discovery that has contributed to the success of her family life. She views marriage as a job, not a "happy-go-lucky rose garden party." It takes hard work. It takes compromise.

And if a new husband, a step-child and an infant weren't enough, Van's family also included ten rescued pets: four dogs, two llamas, two horses, a cat and a rabbit. Since childhood, Van has had a passion for animals. She transformed that passion into a mission. She started a non-profit organization, The Cheyenne Foundation, named after a horse that was almost beaten to death. As a result of Van's efforts, the North Carolina laws were changed to make these kind of animal cruelty cases a felony. Until Van got involved such crimes were only prosecuted as a simple misdemeanor with no possibility for significant punishment or penalty. Van changed that and over the past few years she has personally rescued, rehabilitated and found homes for approximately 120 animals.

Though it hasn't been easy, Van realizes how fortunate she is to be able to live the life that she does. A thriving business, a successful non-profit organization, a husband she truly loves and two amazing children; what more could anyone ask for?

How about a lifetime supply of juicy Angus Barn steaks? Sure, the steaks are great, but good steaks can be had on lots of street corners. What Van truly thrives on is the "personality" of the Angus Barn.

Where else can you meet Rose Beach, a little old lady rocking in the restaurant lobby, and learn that she was the very first employee ever hired by the Angus Barn? Today, more than forty years later, Rose can no longer serve tables. But Van sees value in paying her daddy's first-employee-ever to sit and rock and chat with arriving guests. And the guests see value in that, too, knowing that Van makes sure the way things "used to be" are the way they still are at the Angus Barn.

That's why New York "Snow Birds" who could fly non-stop to Florida go out of their way to connect through the Raleigh-Durham airport just to sit at a table and be served by Van's employees. International travelers from Australia and Japan travel to the area on the promise of a meal at "Big Red." There are thousands of tales of wedding proposals, celebration dinners and graduation parties. Executives who, as nervous boys twenty years ago, came to the Angus Barn to propose to their girlfriends, now travel back from Ohio and Michigan and Colorado with those same sweethearts to celebrate each anniversary. People from all over come to celebrate with their North Carolina family—the staff of the Angus Barn.

They come from down the street and around the world to a big red barn with its own exit sign off the interstate. They arrive in SUVs, airport rental cars, pick up trucks and limousines. On a typical evening, 900 diners come in the front door, each anticipating not only a great meal but a great experience. And on the way out, those same 900, satisfied with both, make a final stop in front of a huge bowl of bright red apples, otherwise known as "Angus Barn dinner mints." Seasoned veterans tell first-time diners: "These are good luck apples. Be sure to take one."

In today's world where it seems there is an "extra charge" for just walking into most places, the $25,000 a year that the Angus Barn spends on "good luck apples" is Van's way of telling her guests: "You're family; please come back soon."

And they do.

DISABLING ════════
BARRIERS

ADRIAN GUGLIELMO ════════
CEO, Diversity Partners
New York, New York

E<small>VERYBODY CAN SHARE</small> a September 11th story, but Adrian Guglielmo, CEO of a business located directly across the street from the World Trade Center, was right there to see that first plane slam into the side of the tower. She was in her car on the way to work when tragedy unfolded right before her eyes. She knew immediately that this was no accident. Remembering the stories told by her husband, a detective in the NYPD, of the aftermath of the first World Trade Center bombing, Adrian could all too clearly see that what was happening in front of her would blow that earlier act of terrorism away. She knew the city would soon be paralyzed by panic.

Adrian's first instinct, the instinct of a mother, was to make sure that her children were safe. Gasping for air, Adrian turned her car around to pick up her three children and bring them home. After that, she could deal with her business and the fate of her employees.

Once at home, Adrian attached herself to the phone, frantically trying to check off names of employees she thought might have been in the building. She didn't stop calling until she had determined that each of her thirteen employees was safe. She sighed in relief when she placed that last call, little knowing the monstrous scope of devastation that would soon unravel.

First, news came of her cousin, Scott Davidson, a fireman. He had been lost in the second tower. Then, bit by bit, Adrian learned the tragic fate of several of her customers with offices in the towers, including those at Windows on the World, the restaurant on the top floor of One World Trade Center. These were people who, over the years, Adrian had come to know as friends.

Last, and certainly least of her concerns at the time, was her office which had been completely destroyed. After five years in business, it seemed that everything she had achieved had disappeared in a blink; that she had been knocked back to the starting gate. All that remained of her thriving business was a single home computer and her AOL account.

Over the next five months, she put her business on the back burner as she tried to make some sense out of life, a life which seemed now to have little or no context. Then the faces of the people who worked for her began to haunt her. These were not your everyday employees. Each of Adrian's thirteen had some form of disability. Each relied on Adrian not only for a job, but also for a sense of independence. In the back of her mind, Adrian began to hear the rumblings of Eva Arnowich, her beloved late grandmother, her beloved *deaf* grandmother, challenging Adrian to continue the important work she had started: to not only rebuild Diversity Partners, but to make it an even better company and provide even more good jobs for a population that so often got the shaft.

And then, as if in need of further motivation, she received a kick in the pants in the form of an email from Bill Donnelly, supplier diversity director of United Parcel Services. "Get off your butt," the email read. "I've got a job for you. We *need* you as a vendor." That day, Adrian began to build the *new* Diversity Partners.

~

In the past, no one in Adrian's life had been more adept at giving her a good kick in the pants when she needed it, than her

Nanny, Eva Arnowich. While Adrian's parents worked during the day, Nanny Eva watched the little girl. A woman of great spirit and motivation, her grandmother, day after day, took what life threw at her and turned it around. Nothing seemed to daunt or stop her. Although uneducated, Nanny, a beautiful Sephardic-looking Jewish woman with black hair draping down to her waist, had managed to marry a highly-educated man.

Proud as she was of her grandmother, not a day went by that Adrian wasn't also embarrassed by her in some form or another. As a kid, Adrian loved to go to the movies, but hated going up to the ticket booth with her grandmother. She always cringed when Nanny would say in the deep guttural voice of the deaf, "I can't hear. I want to pay half." It made perfect sense to Nanny that she should only pay for the visual portion of the movie. Why should she pay for the sound when she couldn't hear it? It wasn't that she couldn't afford the full price; it was that she knew she was in a position to bargain and she loved getting a deal. Of course, she was let in for half price. Embarrassing for her granddaughter? Yes. An important lesson for a future business owner? Unequivocally, yes! Negotiate everything. Get the best deal you can.

The philosophy also worked for Nanny when she was selling. Adrian's father owned several carpet stores, and on a regular basis, Adrian would tag along with Nanny to one of the stores. But whenever a customer came in, Adrian would rush to the other side of the store to hide as Nanny approached the customer and said loudly in her harsh deaf voice, "Please buy carpeting. I'm deaf." Well, what was the customer going to say, "No?" Not to Nanny, he wouldn't. The customer, at a complete loss as to what to do, would buy the carpet.

Adrian was humiliated by Nanny on an almost daily basis, but as she grew up, she realized what an amazingly clever woman her grandmother was. During her time with Nanny, Adrian earned an MBA in "Street Smarts."

Nanny's lessons extended beyond the rules of business and bargaining. Adrian's grandfather, Joseph Arnowich, was also deaf, as were several aunts and uncles. Adrian and her three brothers were taught that Nanny was her grandmother, not her *deaf* grandmother; and that Joseph was her grandfather, not her *deaf* grandfather. Her father had been raised that way as well, never to think of the deafness of his family members as a handicap, but rather as a difference, like right and left handedness; and he passed this mindset on to his children. In Adrian's young mind, Nanny was the strict grandmother, and Grandma Hanna, her mother's mother, was the pushover.

When her Grandma Hanna wanted to correct Adrian, she'd speak to her very politely in Yiddish. Even though Adrian couldn't speak the language, she knew full well what her grandmother was saying. And she'd respond in English. It was the same way with Nanny. Except that Nanny, being more spirited than Grandma Hanna, would yell rather than politely correct Adrian. She'd yell at her in sign language, her hands flying in front of Adrian's face. So, from the perspective of a young child, both of her grandmothers were the same. They each spoke to her in non-English and Adrian understood them both, communicated with them both and loved them both.

Later in life, when Adrian began to add things up, she realized that her childhood community contained as many deaf members as hearing ones. This meant that every family holiday, wedding and Bar Mitzvah always required an interpreter as well as a microphone. Entertainment at these events wasn't reserved for those who could hear. Along with the music, there were magicians and other visual presentations. Once, Adrian and her brother, Harry, dressed up as Harpo and Groucho Marx and pranced around entertaining the group in mime.

So Adrian grew up with an enhanced awareness of all of her senses. To compensate for their lack of speech and hearing, the deaf are typically very tactile. When Nanny wanted to gain her granddaughter's attention, to scold her or to ask her to do a chore, she would shake her—no matter how big Adrian got. Even after Adrian had long surpassed Nanny in height, the older woman would still just come over and shake the younger one and then her hands would start flying with rebuke or directions.

But Nanny also had a gentle, contemplative side. After coming home from the store or finishing the dishes, Nanny would sit on the sofa and pat the seat next to her. This was Adrian's invitation to come join her. Then, they'd sit together, Nanny taking Adrian's young hands into her lap and rubbing her wrists continually, sometimes for half an hour. Whenever they were together, there was a physical closeness, an intimacy.

One of the wonderful elements of being a child in a deaf family was this intimacy. Even Adrian's father, a big, macho man, hugged and kissed each one of his children. This was how he expressed himself because that's what he'd learned from his deaf parents.

～

For Adrian, expressing herself was never the problem. It was containing herself that posed the challenge. For as far back as Adrian could remember, she had been "antsy." It was not until recently that Adrian was diagnosed with Attention Deficit Disorder, a condition not recognized back in the 1960s. She was a horrible student who never could sit still in school. Far worse, she was so hyped up that she never slept. She would stay up all night reading every book in the house. She was a real bookworm, even reading the encyclopedia from A to Z. And always there was a loneliness, a sense of being different, of not being in synch with the rest of the world.

All her teachers told Adrian that she was stupid. "Scraping the bottom of the barrel" was how some put it. The whole time she was in school, Adrian never had a teacher who liked her. They would call her "troublemaker" and say that she "didn't have any respect for authority." At sixteen, she gave up and dropped out of school.

In a time when women didn't pump gas, Adrian took a job at a gas station. That's part of the reason she wanted to work there—because it wasn't done. But after pumping gas for a few weeks, she decided it wasn't the way she wanted to spend her life. So she went back to get her GED. To Adrian's delight, and the amazement of all her teachers, she was able to complete her GED before her class even graduated from high school. And she gained it without studying, which gave her a clearer sense of her intelligence. She wasn't "stupid." In fact, she happened to be downright smart. It was just that she learned things differently than other people.

After completing her GED, Adrian enrolled in the State University of New York at New Paltz. Applying herself to her studies was tough. Adrian's concentration skills were shaky at best. But academics aside, one of the greatest things about her time at New Paltz was that she met her husband, Stephen. He was one good-looking guy. While other girls were baking him cookies and making excuses to sit next to him during study sessions, an equally smitten Adrian tried a different tactic. She focused on the fact that he was a runner. Because she had a high energy level and was an athlete, she knew she could keep up with him. She became his running partner. Then one day while they were studying for a biology test together, she looked him straight in the eye and said, "Shut the book!" That was the moment when friendship became romance.

While in college, Adrian earned money working in her dad's carpet store. The store was located in Manhattan Plaza on 42nd Street and 10th Avenue underneath the Actors' Guild's subsidized apartments. The mix of people in this area reflected the fanfare of 42nd Street. One minute they'd get hookers and drug dealers coming in the door and the next, someone like Harvey Keitel, Jessica Savich or Carol Burnett would step in.

One day while Adrian was alone in the store, a smallish man walked in and asked to see an area rug that was hanging from the very top shelf. Adrian was wearing a short dress that day, and at first, she thought that the customer was just playing with her. But because her father had always encouraged her to "treat every customer as though he were going to spend a million bucks," she went up to get the carpet. She was amazed when he asked if she would take a check. "Sure," she said, as he wrote out the check and handed it to her. In bold letters at the top of the check was the name "Tennessee Williams."

This stopped Adrian in her tracks. She had been to lots of places and had met lots of people. She was a regular at Studio 54 and partied with the best of them, but when it came to writers, she was star struck. As far as she was concerned, Tennessee Williams was the greatest writer who had ever lived. She had read his works by the time she was twelve and reread them by fifteen. His sad, lonely writing had been a nightly companion to this sad, lonely girl. To meet him was to look at her soul in a mirror.

Totally flustered at this surprise encounter with her muse, she looked up at him and said, "Oh my God, you're Tennessee Williams, THE SINGER." Well, that wildly inaccurate comment started him laughing. He laughed so hard that he had to turn away from her. When he finally turned back to look at her, Adrian was mortified. My God, what had just come out of her mouth? The singer? Where did that even come from? Her attempt to redeem herself only made things worse. "Oh, Mr. Williams," she said, "at least you know now that we're not immortal." Well, this crazy statement sent him over the edge. He left the store looking back at her and wiping tears of laughter from his eyes.

As Adrian later learned, Tennessee Williams apparently told this story to his entire literary circle because the following week, the screenplay writer and novelist, William Goldman, wrote a short story about "the girl with the short skirt" who confused Williams with Tennessee Ernie Ford. The whole episode had been "immortal"-ized in Goldman's story.

∾

Adrian may have missed out on her opportunity to have a meaningful encounter with her muse, but she was not going to miss out on having a meaningful experience at college. Trouble concentrating or not, she hung in, sometimes by her fingertips, and ultimately earned a Masters in Psychology. After graduating, she spent years in a variety of drug and alcohol rehab jobs. Although these roles were often satisfying, she felt that something was missing.

Then Nanny died, taking with her the physical intimacy that Adrian had come to count on. Adrian searched for years to fill this void. She tried religion, reaching back to her Eastern European roots. She tried all types of group therapy. She took more school courses. One day, when she was in her early thirties, she visited a graphic arts school for the deaf. The physical closeness of the people she met that day slapped her back to her roots. Oh, my God, she thought, I'm home.

One thing that puzzled her was that not a single one of these obviously talented students had a job. All of the deaf people in Adrian's life had been employed, so she had no way of knowing that eighty percent of the deaf community is unemployed. When she asked these physically capable adults why they weren't working, they looked back at her and eagerly signed the question: "Well, could you get us jobs?" That question sparked an immediate, emotional decision to help them find employment. Adrian proceeded by following up on ads for graphic designers. Even though she had been raised in a deaf family, she was shocked by the prejudice she discovered. She couldn't get anyone to even interview a deaf candidate. She heard excuses like, "Oh they can't answer a phone," or "How am I going to communicate with them?" Adrian was appalled. She decided to leave her quite comfortable job and start a company that would provide jobs for the deaf.

Adrian found a real parallel between her experiences the day she visited the school for the deaf and Robert Kennedy's visit to children in the deep South in the late sixties. Like Bobby Kennedy, one of her great heroes, Adrian came from a wealthy family and had never wanted for anything. Just as he had been sheltered from the fact that the poor were starving, so she was sheltered from the underside of the deaf community. She had been unaware that the deaf were "starving" for jobs, for opportunities, for significance.

Bobby Kennedy's trip into the back roads of the South, the day that he met those children, talked to them, picked them up, and hugged them, was the day that his whole life changed, the day he became the Kennedy who Cared. Adrian's trip to that school, the day she learned the reality of the deaf world, was the day that her whole life changed. Because Kennedy's life was cut short, we'll never know the difference he might have made. But Adrian did have the opportunity to make a difference, and she took it upon herself to change the quality of life for the disabled community all around her.

Early on, Adrian realized that in advertising, the deaf are portrayed more than any other disabled segment. She was aware that a snippet of sign language integrated into a commercial causes an audience reaction of, "Ahh, doesn't that warm your heart?" The same thing happens with print ads of people in wheelchairs; the reader is meant to react, "What a responsible company, they're including the handicapped." These ads may have won points with viewers and readers, but they riled Adrian. How dare these corporations use those with physical impairments to sell their products while choosing not to employ them to create the products? How dare these companies not enhance their products for accessibility?

～

Adrian now had a mission. She developed a totally new concept and created a for-profit business called Diversity Partners. Her creative agency focused on promotional and advertising specialty items, and was staffed entirely by disabled employees. Diversity Partners would allow disabled employees to work for a profitable company just like everyone else. Nonprofits fill a lot of roles, but Adrian felt strongly that they were not good for disabled employees. She could easily have written grant proposals and gained funding, but she wanted to build a "real" company where her employees could play a proud role.

With precious little startup money and three small children at home, Adrian wasn't exactly in the best position to start a new enterprise. Adrian decided a home office would be the way to kick off her new business. On her first day at work she settled herself at her new desk and smiled. Where to begin? Well, she had just gotten her American Express card in the mail. She decided that AmEx would be her first customer. She figured that there would be no problem. Because she was one of their clients, wouldn't they want to be her client?

It took forty-two phone calls to get the name of the right contact person. She then left a message saying that she ran a company employing persons with disabilities. Believe it or not, the phone rang fifteen minutes later. Adrian was in complete shock and totally unprepared to speak with a representative of a corporation like American Express. She hadn't even tried to sell to a small business yet. When the American Express contact asked, "What can I do for you?" Adrian had no idea. She blurted out, "I would love to design your AmEx t-shirts." The contact replied, "What AmEx t-shirts?" There were no t-shirts to be designed, but Adrian managed to convince the American Express rep to meet with her the following week.

The day of the appointment came and Adrian's phone rang. It was what she had feared; her babysitter couldn't make it. Adrian called around. No one could cover for her. She wasn't about to risk losing the meeting by rescheduling. She decided to just bring her toddler along. Already feeling flustered, Adrian looked in her closet to decide what to wear. As a psychotherapist, her business wardrobe consisted of jeans and sneakers. She had no professional clothes at all. So, in her "schmotta," with two-year-old Anthony in tow, she proceeded to American Express Corporate Headquarters in New York City. There, she was led into a boardroom where she found the entire staff of the purchasing department awaiting her.

As she began to explain her offerings, little Anthony decided to "explore" the room. To this day, Adrian bows her head to the sympathetic gentleman from American Express who held her two-year-old on his lap through most of the meeting. Perhaps they felt sorry for her, or perhaps they were impressed by her determination; either way, at the end of the meeting they told her they needed 10,000 mouse pads. She looked at the group quizzically. Did they have a lot of mice in their building? She figured she had better not ask questions. She would just give them what they wanted. Without knowing what she had committed to produce, she had her first order for $20,000. The business was officially launched.

∾

Diversity Partners was off to a strong start, but the pitfalls were soon to reveal themselves. If there were a book called *"How to Make Mistakes While Starting a Business,"* Adrian's picture would be on the cover. From misusing credit cards, to choosing lousy partners, to chasing after the wrong kind of customers, she was the textbook case for how *not* to start a business.

Adrian's naïve sense that she could personally finance all the purchasing she needed almost brought down the business. She takes full responsibility for the disaster caused by her penchant for using her personal credit. She had thought, Why not? The sales would pay her back. She didn't realize that clients can sometimes take a very long time to pay. When she got to the point where she was drowning in debt, she began to wise up. Then, strongly disciplining herself, she dug out of the hole that she had created.

As if poor financial decisions weren't bad enough, Adrian seemed to magnetically attract the wrong partners. She later realized that there was a real potential for business partners to perceive the hook of the company, working with the disabled, as an easy sell, a fast way to make a buck. Her early partners wanted to ride on the backs of the disabled and take advantage of them, rather than sharing Adrian's mission to create careers for talented individuals who were all too often overlooked. Another issue with early partners was their inability to understand that building a business requires extra dedication and long hours. Unfortunately, she partnered with one or two prima donnas before she found a partner who really shared her mission.

That person was Susan Theriot. One day out on a sales call, Adrian was going through her usual pitch about helping individuals with disabilities while providing top-quality, competitively priced goods when she noticed that Susan, the merchandise director, was listening intently. Susan subsequently directed her buyers to do business with Diversity Partners, and some very substantial orders followed. Later Adrian learned that her speech had hit home with Susan, the legal guardian of a disabled sister. Susan and Adrian stayed in touch, and when Adrian parted ways with her previous business partner, Susan came on board. After working in marketing and merchandising for twenty-five years, Susan had finally found the right spot.

Through the whirl of financial difficulties and partners coming and going, Adrian never lost faith in her vision. In fact, she made the opposite mistake. At times, she chased her dreams a little too hard. The mistake she often made in the early years of her company was to go after things that were way beyond her capability. She spun her wheels chasing the wrong projects. The key thing she has learned through these mistakes is to go after work that is reasonable for the size of her company and work her way up from there. It's fine to have dreams, but sometimes she has chased pipedreams.

A classic case was Adrian's introduction to Johnson & Johnson. It was a fiasco on her part. She first bid on a J&J project when Diversity Partners was only a $150,000 company. The project was huge, way outside of her range, but that didn't stop her from responding to J&J's Request for Proposal with a proposal that she killed herself to get out—a 200-page document that she delivered with 290 typos. A flush of embarrassment still flows over Adrian's face every time she thinks of it. She knows now that she had no business even bidding on that job, and the dismal proposal she delivered was proof of that.

At the time, she never expected to hear from J&J again. She certainly didn't deserve to. But about a year later, they gave her the opportunity to work with a smaller division of their company. Rather than the multi-million-dollar deal she originally went after, her first J&J order was for $7,500. Rob Boyce of Independence Technology, a J&J company, said to her, "You work with us, we'll work with you."

In fact, this was the turning point in her business. J&J, starting small, gave Adrian a chance to prove herself. As a result, she now provides an entire catalog of J&J products, including a bag especially designed for the back of the new J&J IBOT wheelchair that goes up steps. The bag is co-branded with the logos of both J&J and Diversity Partners—representing a real partnership. Rob Boyce, proud to have discovered the company for J&J, is one of Diversity Partners' biggest advocates. He is always telling colleagues that they will never find a more passionate company to work with than Diversity Partners.

Adrian may have made some huge mistakes in building her business, but she's made a lot of the right moves as well. Early in the life of Diversity Partners, Adrian had a very simple yet powerful idea. Through her innovative "Give Something Back" program, a portion of the profits from every order is donated to the charity of the client's choice, in the client's honor. By recognizing the needs of her clients to have good community relations and unbeatable public relations, Adrian has figured out a way to get more business while helping support the special communities she most cares about. And clients appreciate it. Adrian received a gift in the words of Avis' VP of Diversity, Lynn Boccio: "I have worked with a number of remarkable people. However, no one shows the compassion and commitment to people with disabilities that Adrian does. I am both touched and inspired as I observe her passion and dedication to their welfare and advancement."

Avis turned out to be another breakthrough client. Adrian first met Lynn at the Women's Business Enterprise National Council (WBENC) Convention where the Avis executive looked her right in the eye and said, "We're going to work with you." Their first project together was a small bubble pen. They've moved up the chain a step at a time to the granddaddy project in which Diversity Partners supports Avis' goal of becoming the most accessible rental car company in the world.

To achieve this goal, Adrian's team develops adaptive equipment for Avis rental cars, enabling people with special needs to use them. Also, Adrian's company is doing the entire marketing and promotional campaign for this project, a project that Adrian's contact at Avis calls the most significant new business launch in Avis' history. Now that's a relationship.

~

Her years in clinical psychology provided Adrian with a storehouse of knowledge on cultivating personal relationships. Psychologists deal with lots of strange things, and one of the strangest things that Adrian learned to deal with is the behavior of serial killers. Amazingly, she has converted this bizarre knowledge into a useful business strategy. According to psychological research, a serial killer only wants to think of you as a number, and the way to throw him off is to have him see you as a real person. If the intended victim blurts out, "My name is Jane. I have three children. My husband loves me. My mother is sick and I tend to her," the killer is exposed to the victim as a person. It is less likely that he'll kill her because he begins to see her as a human being. So, in turn, Adrian believes that it is important for Corporate America to know her as a human being as well as a vendor.

To underscore this belief, Adrian has created her own set of ground rules around her children. Her fourteen-year-old son, Max, often accompanies her to client dinners. And she routinely involves all three of her children in client projects such as a recent New York City marathon event sponsored by Avis. Adrian wants her kids to see it all, and she wants her customers to know she has kids. She believes that this allows clients to look behind the curtain of "Adrian the CEO" to see "Adrian the Person," thus enhancing their relationship.

A buyer with Carvel, the ice cream company, experienced a close encounter with this philosophy on a day when Adrian had two sick children in her office. During the phone conversation, her two kids started screaming. She turned to them and said, "If you'll stop screaming for five minutes, your college education is in the bag." Well, the buyer from Carvel started laughing hysterically. He had kids himself and could well relate to Adrian's situation. She ended up getting the contract.

From her experience as a psychotherapist, she always remembers that everyone is a human being, even big corporate executives. Everyone has the same basic problems, even those in corner offices. Exposure to people from all walks of life, from the famous—remember how she made Tennessee Williams laugh—to her husband's friends in the police department, has taught Adrian to walk into corporate doors as a human being rather than as a vendor.

And throughout her career, it's been about relationships for Adrian. That's her real secret. There is Misha Millon, the Wall Street investment banker, who always tells it like it is, but who never judges. There is Jay Van Vechten, the consummate PR pro, who has guided Adrian through sometimes muddy corporate waters; directed much business her way; and is always there for advice, good cheer and support, often via late-night, instant messaging.

These relationships proved especially critical when Adrian began the daunting task of rebuilding her business after her office was destroyed in the World Trade Center attack. Many old friends were there to support the phoenix rising from the ashes. And many new relationships were forged. A critically important one was with Bob Notine. After only two meetings with Adrian, Bob agreed to come on board as a partner, giving the company the critical financial support it needed to get back on its feet. But more than providing financial backing, Bob has been there any time Adrian has needed straight-up, on-the-money advice.

As Adrian developed a plan to get back on track, she realized that this national tragedy had wiped the slate clean for her. Every mistake she had made in her business had been relegated to the past. This disaster gave her the opportunity to rethink her position as a CEO; reorganize her business and her personal life; and rebuild her business in a location only ten minutes from her home in Westchester. Adrian has become a better person and a better businesswoman as a result.

∽

While building and then rebuilding her business, Adrian has received all kinds of recognition. However, she knew that she had arrived when WBENC asked her to speak in front of 1,000 businesswomen at a breakfast meeting. To her left sat "The Businesswoman of the World" and to her right was a woman with a three-billion-dollar business. These women were eloquent speakers and somehow the speech that Adrian had prepared began to seem inappropriate. When it was her turn to speak, Adrian mentally threw out her prepared speech. She stood up and just spoke from her heart. She told the women that starting a business was like walking across hot coals. She shared with them the good, the bad, and the ugly without any sugarcoating. She talked about what it was like to create the new Diversity Partners after her office was destroyed in the terrorist attack. At the conclusion, Adrian received a standing ovation and two new corporate clients.

From that experience, Adrian learned that she shouldn't try to change. Over the years, people have advised her to change her appearance, tone down her Brooklyn accent and calm down a little. But she has learned that she is successful because her appearance and attitude make her different and unique. When they see her, her friends playfully call out, "Yo, Adrian." It is more than a play on the movie, *Rocky*. There are real similarities between Adrian and the famous boxer. She is willing to work and work and work and not let up. And she expects to win. And when she does, she will win not only for herself, but also for all those who are, like her, a little different.

Adrian's vision has never been to give people "jobs," but rather to enable them to gain a full set of business skills so that they can become professionals with real careers. Employees of Diversity Partners attend meetings with Microsoft, McDonald's, Avis and UPS. They design logos, develop product concepts and keep the office humming behind the scenes. At Diversity Partners, it is about "ability," never "disability."

From her initial plan to provide jobs for the deaf, Adrian expanded Diversity Partners to include the developmentally disabled and those in wheelchairs. She provides these people with serious careers, not just a check. She puts real demands on her employees, expecting them to be on time and produce high quality deliverables. As a result, employees of Diversity Partners experience something most of us take for granted, but something that is unusual in the special needs community— a real sense of fulfillment.

In many organizations, disabled people are spoiled; they are taught that their wheelchair or deafness excludes them from corporate rules. While these corporations have good intentions, Adrian believes they are "enablers" of sorts, because they don't expect the disabled to perform as well as those without disabilities. Diversity Partners has extraordinary expectations of all its employees, and the employees know they have to carry their own weight. That doesn't mean that people are expected to do things beyond their physical capabilities. That wouldn't be reasonable. Rather, employees are given the opportunity to expand to the full limit of their capabilities. And Diversity Partners' employees will tell you that this solves their problems much better than a monthly check from the government. This provides equal footing to a group of individuals who have long been shortchanged in so many aspects of their lives.

One of these areas is wrapped around the American dream—purchasing a home. It might be just a check on the to-do list of life for most middle-Americans, but home ownership is a rare thing for disabled individuals. So it is a day of great celebration for everyone at Diversity Partners when an employee moves into his or her own home. This move is significant not only for the new homeowner, but as a form of encouragement for all fellow workers, because it provides a sense that each of them can take the next step towards a fulfilling life.

Before meeting Adrian, many of these individuals would have been grateful for a dead end job stocking groceries. Now they are challenged to use their full creative and technical abilities to exist independently and live their lives to their fullest potential.

And through her mission, Adrian is also challenged to live her life to its fullest potential. With her business back on track and in the black, she has one more goal. Her ultimate dream is to stand on the floor of NASDAQ and announce in sign language, the first public company run by and for people with disabilities. Knowing Adrian, it is just a matter of time.

BREAKING
THE BONDS

MARCIA REYNOLDS

President, Covisioning
Phoenix, Arizona

RUSSIAN FAIRY TALES and folk songs had colored her childhood. But Marcia Reynolds also grew up in the shadow of a true tragedy. Her grandparents escaped the Bolshevik revolution in 1916. As a newly married couple, just fourteen- and fifteen-years-of-age, they left Russia to immigrate to America. Penniless, they arrived in Cleveland to carve out a new life for themselves. They never heard from a single member of their family again. Mothers, fathers, brothers, sisters, aunts, uncles, cousins—all gone.

In November 2002, Marcia became the first in her family to return to her grandparents' homeland. This was no ordinary trip. Marcia was there to speak at the first-ever coaching conference in Russia. Although she had given speeches to coaches and would-be coaches at conferences in all corners of the globe, this speech was different. This was the place where her family had suffered. These were the people she had most wanted to touch.

Marcia stepped up to the podium. *"Spokini nochy, vnuchen'ka,* Goodnight, my granddaughter," Marcia whispered hoarsely into the microphone. "My grandmother used to say those words to me."

As she delivered her speech in front of a crowd of 200 people, Marcia found herself choking up. She talked about a personal coach's power to open people's eyes to the possibilities in their lives. A fairly new idea in America, personal coaching is a revelation in a country like Russia. Marcia saw people in her audience tearing up as she talked about how, as a coach, she could help people become aware of their emotions, their pains, their fears, their anger and their joy and through this new sense of self-awareness create a life of great happiness.

Marcia, a well-traveled, well-heeled, privileged American, may have seemed like an unlikely source to be lecturing on how to lead a joyful life to a people who only were beginning to learn what it was like to lead a life free of shackles. How could Marcia, a woman who seemed to have been born with everything, truly understand the struggle of people who had been free only a decade after centuries of oppression?

She couldn't. All she could do was put forward the lessons she had learned in an unlikely place from an unlikely coach.

~

That unlikely place was Maricopa County Jail. It was June 1976, one month before Marcia's twentieth birthday, when Marcia's mother dropped her off in front of the jailhouse. A heroine addict facing up to seven years in prison, Marcia was beat, broke and out of hope.

"Be a good girl," Marcia's mother said hugging her at the curb. She tucked a stray dark strand of hair behind her daughter's ear. Marcia swatted her hand away.

Marcia's legs shook as she walked into the jailhouse with her toothpaste and a comb. Less than an hour later, clad in a shapeless dark blue smock, she breathed in the stale, sweaty air of her new home: cell #6. And she began the journey that was to turn her life around.

The start of Marcia's adventure was marked by pain, fear, fever and excruciating need. She lay in her bunk shivering, sweating and moaning in the throes of heroine withdrawal. Her four cellmates, a blur of dark faces and blue smocks, took turns keeping vigil over her. They knew what this was about. They had been there before. But after three days, when Marcia finally, blissfully fell into a real sleep, the empathy ended. An angry voice woke her up: "Get back to your own bed, white girl."

Marcia spent the next few days curled up in her bunk, gazing out through the steel bars, trying to figure out what had gone wrong. She fantasized that her father was on his way to pick her up. Her father, Sam A. Charns; funny, controlling, a community theater star, an accomplished entrepreneur. He stood on center stage in both her family life and in their small, Jewish community in Phoenix, Arizona. Sam told people that his middle initial stood for "Almighty." He told Marcia that she was better than anyone else. And she spent her childhood doing everything in her power to prove him right.

A top student, a star athlete, a member of student council, the class smart aleck, a favorite of the cutest boys, Marcia did a pretty good job of grabbing attention in grade school. But everything changed when she started high school in 1969. A school board experiment pulled Marcia out of the class she had been with since first grade—the smart kids—and put her into another class—the not-as-smart kids.

Marcia wondered why she had been booted from her class. Had she suddenly become stupid? Her confidence shot, Marcia did what she could to take her place at the top of this class. But here, the rules of the game were different. Instead of grades and sports, Marcia quickly intuited that the path to acceptance and popularity was drugs and sex. Again, Marcia outdid her classmates.

When the experiment in "integration" didn't work, the board put Marcia back into her old class, but it was too late. She had faced a difficult situation by doing what she'd been taught to do: be the best, take center stage. But this time her actions had not made her happy. They had left her confused and in trouble, lonely and angry—damn angry. She had lost her place and her faith in herself. She was tired of being pushed around. A rebellion bubbled up inside her. Unable to process her intense anger, Marcia passed her days in a haze of LSD, marijuana, barbiturates and methamphetamine.

Fifteen-year-old Marcia met Ronnie in a drug program. Both teens were attending the drug program under pressure from their parents. Both teens ignored the messages of the program, but did not ignore the messages of their hearts. They fell for each other. Ronnie always knew the exact moment to rub Marcia's neck and kiss her nose. And he knew that Marcia could deny him nothing. Not even her veins.

The needles terrified Marcia, but Ronnie threatened to leave her if she didn't share the experience with him. Marcia was violently ill the first time Ronnie shot heroine into her arm. Her body rejected it, but boy oh boy, did she want more: the warmth going through her body, the darkness, the peace.

Even a heroine addiction could not slow Marcia down in high school. She graduated sixth out of her class of 300. Well respected for her stash of prime Columbian marijuana and for her quick, witty dialogue, she had maintained star status in high school. But following graduation, she couldn't cut it as a star in the streets.

Marcia gave up a full scholarship to Northern Arizona University. For the next three years, her life was all about two things: getting drugs and taking drugs; in other words, begging, stealing, smuggling, copping and shooting.

There were moments of diversion. Like when her boyfriend smacked her around. When a woman died in her arms from an overdose. When she almost died from an overdose herself— twice. Once she was even declared dead and had the sheet pulled over her head.

Marcia made fleeting attempts to stabilize her life. She managed to pass a few college courses. She married Ronnie. But three months into the marriage, both Ronnie and Marcia were busted on possession charges. Marcia took the rap and got probation. Her father committed her to a drug program at a mental hospital, and Ronnie disappeared. One month later,

Marcia signed herself out of the hospital and was back on the streets.

Marcia grew tired—tired of telling lies, tired of fearing that her friends might cheat her, tired of waking up in the morning and crawling to her stash, tired of spilling hundreds of dollars worth of drugs onto the carpet before she could get any into her shaking arms. She was too tired to even argue when a snitch named names to save himself. It was her third offense and it brought her to jail cell #6 where she sat, scared and alone, idly tracing her ragged fingernails over the yellow stains on her thin, jail-issued blanket. She sat there with four other sad, angry women in a room the size of her parent's bathroom and wondered how a nice, middle-class Jewish girl, Sam A. Charn's daughter, could have sunk so low.

Marcia's forced jail-time sobriety eventually brought her out of her drug-induced stupor, but it was Vicki, a big, black prostitute and the leader of the biggest, meanest gang in the jail, who truly brought Marcia back to the world of the living.

In her first few months in jail, a frightened Marcia won over many of her fellow inmates. She put to work the same tricks that had worked so well for her in elementary school. She was funny, audacious with the authorities and full of outrageous antics. She made them laugh. Her heart-felt poetry cracked their hard exteriors.

But it was her courage that first caught Vicki's eye. Marcia became a minor celebrity among her inmates after she stood up for Carmella, her cellmate. The drama began when Carmella heard through the jailhouse phone—a toilet that had been hand-plunged of water—that her younger brother had hung himself in an upstairs cell in the men's section. Carmella lost it. Crying and screaming, she could not be calmed down. Alarmed by Carmella's hysterics, three male guards rushed into the cell and pinned her to the bars. When Carmella cried out for help, Marcia started yelling and screaming and jumped up—straight into a guard's fist.

Her defense of Carmella landed her in isolation where, with no idea that her rebellion was being celebrated from cell to cell, Marcia hit rock bottom. She dragged her battered body into the corner and closed her weeping eyes. Her life had no value. She prayed to die.

Then a song, Elton Johns' "Someone Saved My Life Tonight," spilled out of the speakers onto the catwalk. Marcia lifted her head to listen closely to the words. The words "sweet freedom" drifted to her ears. She flashed back to a vision of herself as a child running as fast as she could, laughing out loud. Marcia's eyes popped open. She cringed at the sight of the bars. She looked down at her bruised, frail body. Suddenly, pure rage overwhelmed her. "Stop it, you people trying to take my life," she cried out, reaching through the bars to raise a fist to the ceiling. "It's my life!"

Marcia lay down on the cement and started doing frantic sit-ups and push-ups, relishing the rush of strength surging through her black-and-blue body. Stumbling and cursing, she goaded herself on. Jumping jacks. Running in place. She could not be taken down so easily. She *would* not be taken down so easily.

~

After release from isolation, Marcia enjoyed her new status—mostly because she had won the approval of "Queen Vicki." And Vicki, who dubbed her the "brave little white girl who stood up to the man," was soon transferred into her cell. Vicki strutted in, sat down next to Marcia on her lower bunk and said, "I got a deal for you, Little Bit. I'm kinda big and fat and don't climb up the bunk too well. But I know you earned your bed. So I say we share. I get the bottom bunk three days, then you get it three, and we rotate like that until one of us is outta here."

Needless to say, Marcia never got her bunk back. She didn't care. Their friendship bloomed over the next few months, fanned by vicious games of gin rummy, infestations of lice and battles with the reigning officer of the women guards, the hated Lieutenant Davis.

Vicki was also there for her when, after three months in jail, Marcia's court date finally came up. Facing a possible sentence of up to seven years of prison time, Marcia celebrated with Vicki when the judge, influenced by a letter Marcia had written to him, went against Marcia's probation officer's recommendation and sentenced her to only six months in jail.

Throughout it all, Marcia loved to watch twenty-four-year-old Vicki in action. She lived life to its fullest—even when her world was no bigger than a cage. She said things that the other inmates only felt, bellowed in rage while others skulked in their bunks. She put herself on the line and would rush to the defense of any of "her women."

Vicki's women were not her lovers in a physical sense, but the bonds that held these women together did run deep. Intense friendships grew quickly. Enemies were made just as fast. Jail inmates faced a choice: they could either turn *to* each other or *on* each other. The women lived three to seven to a cell in a windowless space with just enough room for a toilet, a sink and two to four bunk beds. In jail, not a moment is private— not a sob, not a laugh, not a trip to the toilet. Unlike prison, jails are basically seen as warehouses. Programs and resources are scant. The women were typically let out of their cells for an average of two hours a day for showers, visitors and television—that is if the cellblock was not too overcrowded.

One particularly hot day, Marcia and her cellmates learned that a prostitute bust would soon have the jail flooded with inmates. Rather than going through the bureaucratic hassle of opening up a new cellblock, the decision was made to overcrowd Marcia's block and put them all on lockup for at least a week. That meant no showers. No visitors. No television. No breaks from the cell at all. They would be like rats in a cage.

The women were furious, Vicki most of all. Seeing Vicki struggle to contain her fury, Marcia developed an idea for a nonviolent protest. Vicki balked, "You think you can change the rules?"

"Maybe not," Marcia said, "but I can at least call their hand."

Vicki nodded slowly. Marcia began the preparation. She yelled out to the inmates through the catwalk: "Are you angry about the loss of free time? Are you sick of sweaty bodies holed up with no showers? Do you want to be able to see your visitors? Are you tired of being stared at by tour groups? Do you need to see a doctor or a dentist or a counselor?" A chorus of "yes" and "amen sister" followed each question she asked.

Marcia explained the plan and the stage was set. When Vicki heard the key unlocking the catwalk door, she began to kick the wall. The rest of the inmates soon joined her. Female guards came out yelling. The noise intensified as Marcia's chant of "Captain, Captain" echoed through the cellblock.

A male voice finally boomed down the catwalk. "Girls?" the captain said, making his approach accompanied by Lieutenant Davis, "Quiet!"

Lieutenant Davis led the captain straight to Vicki. "All right, Vicki," the captain said. "What's going on?"

Marcia protested, "What do you mean, Vicki? She didn't start this. You did."

Vicki jumped up. "Why are we on restriction? Why can't we shower?"

"We want answers," Marcia said.

"There are reasons," the captain said. "We're severely understaffed and overcrowded."

"Bull," Vicki said.

Voices hollered, "Tell 'em, Vicki," and, "They're lying."

Speaking loudly enough for all the inmates to hear, the captain said, "You're out of line, all of you. The restriction stays."

Vicki unbuttoned her dress. The others followed, ripping off their dresses and tossing them onto the catwalk. The captain moved in front of the dayroom and out of sight. "Stop this," he said.

The inmates threw their trash onto the catwalk. "That's it!" said the captain. As he stormed out five guards rushed in and aimed straight for Vicki. Marcia saw a guard's hand reach back on his belt for his stick.

"No!" Marcia yelled. She leaped like a cat, claws and teeth bared, pushing, scratching, biting. The stick was turned on Marcia. She was punched in the stomach and pinned from behind. Kicking and wailing, Vicki and Marcia were pulled out of their cell and tossed into isolation.

Marcia lay down flat on the cement floor. The two women slowly began to move, wiping away blood from their faces, tentatively wiggling bruised, battered limbs beginning to come back to life. Marcia started to cry. "Sorry," she said. "I didn't know. So stupid. My whole life . . ." But Vicki jumped up, smashing her palm into Marcia's chest and pinning her against the wall.

"Stop it," she said. She put her face into Marcia's. "You are not a loser. You are smart. You are strong. And for some reason known only to God, you care about people. When you get that here," she said, pointing to her heart, "you'll get out of here," she said pointing to the door.

Stunned, Marcia sank to the ground. Then she heard a strange sound like the beat of a tribal drum. "What's that?" she gasped.

Vicki grabbed Marcia's hand and squeezed. "Hah. You did it after all, girl. Can't you hear it?"

Marcia pressed her ear to the wall. The drum beat out names, "Vicki, Marcia, Vicki, Marcia."

The next day, all the women—except Vicki and Marcia—were moved to a larger cellblock. Vicki and Marcia were escorted to a separate cellblock for inmates who were separated from the general population. The cell they shared was equipped with its own shower and television. "Girl, it's the Taj Mahal," said Vicki. Vicki and Marcia spent two months alone in the cell together.

～

When her six months were up, Marcia left the jail, tears streaking her cheeks as Vicki's goodbye echoed in her ear, "I never want to see you again. The only thing I want to see of you is your name in print. You are the one who could make a difference."

At that moment, for the first time, Marcia felt that she had a life purpose. She knew exactly what Vicki was asking. Marcia was in a unique position. She had the background, the schooling and the support that her fellow inmates lacked. She could tell their stories. And maybe she could change the way people are treated in jail. Maybe she could make a difference in people's lives.

Marcia never did see Vicki again. Over the years, fearing the worst, she tried to track Vicki down. Vicki had talked about moving to California where it was easier to be a prostitute. But Marcia couldn't find a clue as to her whereabouts. Vicki had simply disappeared.

Nonetheless, Marcia carried Vicki with her every day. She had copied down the words Vicki spoke to her after the protest: "You're smart. You're strong. You care." Marcia took that piece of paper everywhere. From that day forward, anytime Marcia started to doubt herself, those words boosted her back up. They became her foundation, her bedrock. They made her believe in herself. And she relied heavily on that foundation over the next few years.

Under the direction of the court, Marcia was required to enter a year-long drug program in Nevada. The program was a joke. Drugs were literally being sold outside the back door. Although the temptation became almost unbearable, Marcia held strong. After six months, she couldn't take it anymore and ran away. Facing the prospect of doing seven years in prison,

Marcia promised her probation officer that if they gave her this chance, she would pull her life together. Her probation officer thought she would hang herself, but Marcia knew she could finally break free.

Back in Phoenix, she enrolled in Arizona State University. At twenty-one, Marcia wasn't much older than the other students, but the difference felt like decades. Socially, she hovered on the outside. Academically, she worked with a fervor that turned to obsession. When her journalism classes proved to be the only courses where she had to struggle to score a straight A, she became a journalism major and dug even deeper into her books.

One day coming down the elevator in the library, a small African-American student jumped in the elevator with her. "Take a bath," he said, staring her in the eye.

"What?" Marcia replied in shock.

"I know what you're doing," he said. "I used to work in the jail. You're ok now. Relax. Don't open a book this weekend. Take a warm bath."

He hopped off the elevator as quickly as he had jumped on. Marcia walked home slowly. It was true. She hadn't been taking care of herself. She had been burying her life in her books. She had found yet another way to wear the shackles. She took his advice. She went home and took a long, hot bath.

Slowly, day by day, week by week, hope started to take root. Marcia built a social life, a life that did not have anything to do with drugs. She began to lose the habit of waking up in the morning and longing for her stash of heroine. Instead she would wake up and wonder: could this be the day something incredible happens?

~

Just two years after her release from jail, Marcia was well on her way to graduating *summa cum laude* with a degree in mass communications. She petitioned the court to be released from her probation, at which point her conviction would drop from felony to misdemeanor status—a status change Marcia knew would make all the difference in her job hunt. She needed a good job to save money for graduate school, but as a felon, she faced discrimination everywhere she turned for employment. Sandra Day O'Connor, then an Arizona Superior Court Judge, denied Marcia's request. She said that the rules could not be bent; Marcia was not a "qualified risk."

So Marcia lied on her next application and got the job she needed to continue her studies. Her graduate school work in communication arts focused on using video to help drug addicts and prison inmates improve their self-esteem and communication skills. Marcia wanted to offer an alternative to twelve-step programs. She knew these programs could be effective for many people, but they had simply not worked for her. Declaring herself powerless and an addict all of her life did not ring true for Marcia. What did work was declaring herself powerful. In jail, Marcia forgave herself for her fears, her selfishness, her deceitfulness, her impulsiveness. She embraced her strengths: her compassion, her creativity, her humor and her success orientation. This formula had worked for her and she wanted others to benefit from it.

The power of self-awareness came to life even further for Marcia as she tested video feedback with inmates at San Quentin. She was amazed by the behavioral shifts she saw after only two to three sessions. Marcia tried to carry on this work after graduate school, but the jail and prison decision-makers turned her down. One woman told her to quit feeling guilty and get on with her life. Oh yeah, Marcia replied in her head to the woman. You just wait. I will make something of myself and then you will have to listen to me.

Marcia took a job in a mental hospital as an audio/visual coordinator. After putting in five years, she had hit a dead end. Her inspiration was sapped. The money was bad. She had lost her spark.

She was ready for something new. She took a corporate position in a training department and soon after she started, her boss decided to start a doctorate program, dumping the entire executive training program in Marcia's hands. Marcia panicked, thinking, Me, train executives? What do I know about training corporate executives? Vicki's words came back to her: "You're smart. You're strong. You care." Marcia steadied her nerves and took on the challenge. She enrolled in a Masters program in Educational Psychology and rolled up her sleeves.

Designing and leading training courses was just her speed. She savored being on stage. She enjoyed exploring and sharing what she had learned. Marcia realized that there were many different ways of "giving back." She had found her passion.

Marcia moved into a number of different training positions in the fast paced high-tech industry. She often had to fight her way to the top in the male-dominated, high-tech world, but at this point, a good scrap could hardly cramp her style. Marcia relished using her voice as an agent of change, helping management to see that if they wanted greater productivity, they had to respect and develop the people who did the work.

In 1989, after a management change resulted in an executive team that didn't mesh with her values, Marcia left her job. She tried to help a former colleague get a consulting business off the ground. Yet again, her dreams and values did not mesh with her partner's. So out of work and short on cash, Marcia set out in search of her dream job, one where she could make the difference she knew was possible.

That job appeared in 1990 in the form of Microchip Technology, a semiconductor company on the brink of bankruptcy. The deal she made with the executives was this: Marcia would take care of the people; they would take care of the product and marketing. Marcia put together a training program that lit a fire under the employees. By 1993, the company went public and earned the title of the top IPO in the country for that year.

Many millionaires were made. Marcia did not count among them. Her stock options were good, but would take four years to vest. Marcia decided she couldn't wait. She quit the company after two years, taking a little over $300,000 with her. She left behind about a million dollars in unvested stock. Everyone told her she was crazy. But Marcia knew it was the sanest thing she had ever done. How could she put a price on happiness?

Sure, her job had its perks. She made a lot of money. She traveled the world. But one of Marcia's cherished dreams, having more time to write, seemed to drift farther and farther out of reach. The higher she climbed up the corporate ladder, the less control she had over her time. As Marcia's projects piled up, so did her frustration, stress and anger. She often came home angry or in tears. She didn't even have time to work those emotions off at the gym. She seemed to get sick a lot and her friends, including her boyfriend, were giving up on her. Finally, when her manager denied her last request for a promotion, claiming her position wasn't one that the company could justify raising to the executive level, Marcia had had enough. The company had never promoted a woman to vice president. She doubted they ever would. She had hit another dead end.

～

Marcia still felt she had things to say. She wanted people to listen. She wanted to give back, in a bigger way, the gifts that she had been given. She redrew her life purpose: to help people see life as an adventure full of possibilities.

Marcia started her own firm, Covisioning, in October 1995. She chose the company's name by defining the business' purpose: to work with people and organizations to create happier, healthier lives. Marcia accomplishes this mission with her clients in a special partnership she calls covisioning.

Marcia created covisioning at Microchip Technology as a process designed to help employees within a team create a shared vision. She then expanded the process to align departments through shared visioning. Eventually, she discovered that covisioning was useful anytime two or more people needed to blend expectations and accomplish something together. Marcia has used this process to covision family vacations, product development plans, corporate initiatives, business partnerships and marriages.

Much of Marcia's business is wrapped around teaching a concept called emotional intelligence. The idea is that there are no bad emotions. Fear can protect you. Anger can spur you to great things. Rather than hurting you, emotions, if you understand them, can give you critical information to make better choices and become a better person.

Marcia had messages she wanted to teach, but she needed to perfect how she delivered them. She knew she could support herself solely doing what she had been doing for the past sixteen years. Management development and communication skills training programs and classes would always be a mainstay for her business. But Marcia looked at three additional ways she could grow her own business.

The first was public speaking. Marcia joined the National Speakers Association to learn the business. She worked with a number of acting coaches to hone her craft. It wasn't long before she was speaking at conferences and meetings across the country and around the world.

Over the years, Marcia has addressed diverse groups of people—from corporate executives to high school kids to jail inmates. Her topics all revolve around a single theme: how to see the possibilities in life. Marcia's audiences hear her stories of how she triumphed over adversity; how she failed, many times, and yet continued to pick herself back up again; and how she learned in jail who she was and what she wanted to be in this world. Marcia shares techniques she has learned over the years to stay confident, upbeat and focused. She tells people they are okay. She touches people, and they respond. After one speech to a large audience of Girl Scouts, one of the girls gave

Marcia the book she had been reading, *Touched by an Angel*, and signed it, "To Marcia, a true angel on Earth."

Marcia loved working with groups, but she also saw the power in one-on-one work. She recognized that change takes place over time. Having someone to talk to, to support you and to help you deal with obstacles along the way can help make desired changes a reality. While at Microchip Technology, Marcia had read an article about a woman who served as a personal coach for managers and people wanting to improve their lives—a very new idea at the time.

On the day she resigned, one of the vice presidents came into Marcia's office and quietly asked, "Who will I talk to after you leave? Can I call you?"

Marcia wasn't too happy about the idea, but then he said the magic words, "I'll pay you." Remembering the article, Marcia thought, Alright, I'm a coach! She enrolled in a coaching school to learn how to get started in this other focal area of her business.

Within three months, the two largest newspapers in Phoenix wrote articles about Marcia's coaching practice and she appeared on two local news shows. People started to sit up and take notice. Marcia's first coaching client outside of her Microchip Technology colleagues was Jim, the owner of a law firm. Jim was unhappy with his practice and was contemplating abandoning it altogether to become a high school teacher. Marcia asked him to wait ninety days before taking action and to use that time to explore his needs and identify the intolerable aspects of his business. During this "time-out," Jim recaptured why he had become an attorney twenty years ago: to meet his needs for helping others, to feel important and to have a job that challenged him to grow. Though these motivations were still being fulfilled, the responsibilities of owning a business were weighing him down. Jim tried paring down his business, but when this action didn't cut deep enough, he finally left the business altogether and became a county prosecutor.

This might have been seen as a step down to some, but to Jim, it was heaven. He kept his passion for his work while cutting out the stresses and frustration that had kept him from being happy and fulfilled.

As Marcia developed more and more success stories, she became active in the International Coach Federation. She served as the president in 2000. That year marked her first interviews by national media. Marcia appeared in magazines and newspapers throughout the United States including *Fortune Magazine, Health Magazine, The New York Times* and *Industry Week*. As her fame grew, she began coaching clients by phone around the world.

Marcia was thrilled to see her business grow, but it was her client successes that truly excited her. She was making a real difference in people's lives. Her clients reported increased confidence and energy levels, better clarity in their decision-making and an improved ability to work with others. Overall, they got more satisfaction out of life.

Marcia received another unexpected gift from her coaching career. She found she had tapped into a warm and giving worldwide community of coaches. Although she continued as a sole practitioner, she no longer felt alone.

In addition to management training, speaking engagements and one-on-one coaching, Marcia began pursuing her other dream: to be published. Her first work was a two-cassette audio program entitled *Being in the Zone*. The tapes tell listeners how to maximize their talents to perform at their personal best. *Being in the Zone* then inspired *Golf in the Zone* and later *Tennis in the Zone*.

Her first book, *Capture the Rapture*, published in 2000, tells readers how to move from "existing" to fully "living" their lives. She explains to readers how to create a vision and act on it rather than suffering the frustration of standing still. "Existing," she writes, "lacks enjoyment. Living brims over with enchantment. In a sense all of our lives are spent waiting for something. We save money to go to school; we work so that we can retire; then we proceed with caution so as to live longer. My mother, who all her life repressed her desires, asked to be cremated so that her money would not be spent frivolously. If she were here now, I'd take her dancing."

Marcia then penned her second book, *How to OutSmart Your Brain: Using Your Emotions to Make the Best Decisions.* The book focused on her work in emotional intelligence in the workplace.

One of Marcia's greatest moments of triumph came when she had lunch with her former boss three years after she had left her job at Microchip Technology. He asked if she was struggling. Marcia was glad to tell him that in the previous year she had made more than double the salary she had left behind and had never had to touch her savings. She now had an assistant working for her and was licensing trainers and coaches to teach her class, *Accessing Emotional Intelligence.* Her old boss told Marcia that he was terribly overweight, unhappy in his marriage, mad at his employees and spent most of his time hiding. Marcia knew this man had made millions in the stock market. Again she had to ask herself, how can you price happiness?

As her career took off, the pieces of her personal life also fell into place. Soon after moving into a new house, Marcia took a sharp breath as she realized that everything in her beautiful new home belonged to her. Her parents were now gone. She had just come out of a five-year relationship. She had no man to lean on and even with her many friends, she had no one to financially fall back on if she needed to. The thing was she didn't need to; she was totally self-sufficient. She had learned the real taste of freedom.

It kept getting better. In 2002, Marcia bought another home with a separate guesthouse that houses her business. Her verdant yard offers a lush, private retreat. Her home features a room large enough to hold small classes so she can have people come to her to learn instead of always having to travel to share her ideas. At night, she can lock the door behind her and maintain her life.

Although Marcia's purpose stays the same, she finds the nature of her business is in constant flux. Her business plan is to live comfortably in this mystery, trusting that she will stay successful. Every time she tries to plan her work, new and interesting opportunities arise demonstrating that her planning efforts were largely a waste of time. Instead, she chooses to stay in the moment, weighing opportunities as they show up to see if they fit her purpose and appear to be a good investment of her time. She makes sure all her choices feel as though they will be fun and fulfilling. With this strategy, her business has grown every year.

And Marcia continues to wake up every morning thinking this might be the day something incredible happens.

THE QUEEN
OF BARBEQUE

DONNA MYERS
President/CEO, DHM Group, Inc.
Colts Neck, New Jersey

DONNA MYERS has always liked to eat. Her mother, a homemaker, enjoyed filling the plump, appreciative child with nutritious home cooking. To save money, most of the ingredients were grown in the family garden. Everything was made from scratch. No preservatives. No junk food. Just good, hearty Midwestern fare.

Food played a dominant role in the Scandinavian culture of Minot, the small town in North Dakota where Donna grew up. For any event that would crop up—a birth, a death, a church social, a remodeled kitchen—neighbors would run over bearing a casserole. A child home for a weekend from college was a great excuse to pull out the recipes. "Mom, please. Enough," Donna would beg when she visited from North Dakota State University.

So what did Donna study when she went off to college? What else? Home Economics. But Donna wasn't about to take fluff courses. So she got special permission to take the same chemistry, biology, physics and anatomy and physiology courses as the pharmacy students rather than the watered down versions on the home economics curriculum. Did she struggle with the courses? Yes. Did she regret her decision? No. When she hit a snag, she stayed after class to ask the professor for extra help. Tough as it was, giving up was no option. She was there to learn.

Donna was the typical first child; always a bit of an overachiever. She had a real take-charge attitude. Although sports were never her thing and she wasn't about to be named home-coming queen, she did like to stand out. She expressed herself through things like music and public speaking. In high school she appeared on a weekly hometown TV show, moderated by a minister, which featured teens talking about issues they were struggling with in their lives. Because this was the early 1950s, the show covered topics like whether or not the kids should be allowed to go out of town for sports events or how to handle the situation if someone showed up with beer at a party.

The TV show may not have been a national hit, but it did help Donna cultivate her ability to think on her feet—a skill that came in handy when she finished college and began working for Columbia Gas of Ohio, a public utility that sold natural gas. The general manager of the organization seemed to work twenty-four hours a day. He was magically omnipresent. He taught Donna the meaning of dedication and the infectious nature of passion. She wanted to succeed for his sake, to help him and to make him proud of her. So Donna kept up with his pace.

She faced a formidable task: her job was to sell Ohio on the wonders of gas. No joke. She wrote a column for the local paper, demonstrated gas refrigerators and stoves at ladies' luncheons, talked up gas grills at the Republican clam bake, trained appliance dealers to sell more effectively and peddled the virtues of gas lines to new apartment complexes. She enjoyed the public nature of her job, but after three years of eighty-hour-plus work weeks, Donna realized that if she had to smile at one more customer over one more gas appliance, her head would explode.

She was ready to move on. Donna had always had a fascination with California—a lifestyle she imagined would be much more exciting than that of America's Heartland. She started sending her resume out to the West Coast. Then fate sent her in the opposite direction.

$\sim$

While attending a conference in New York City, Donna met Charles Myers. The girl was smitten. The lovebirds visited back and forth between New York and Ohio. Then, in 1963, Donna took the plunge. She found an apartment in Queens, New York and accepted a position with Best Foods, a manufacturer of brands like Skippy peanut butter and Hellman's mayonnaise.

Though her personal life and career fell into place, Donna experienced unbelievable culture shock. She couldn't fathom why everyone in New York City was so rude, so impersonal and so rushed. For weeks, Donna was mystified by people's need to push and shove in order to stand on one particular spot to catch the subway. She eventually understood that they were vying to stand where the doors would open, but it still didn't make sense to her. *She* didn't push and shove. *She* still got on the train just like everybody else. The grocery store was another puzzle. People were just plain mean. Once, a woman snatched the last can of Campbell's mushroom soup out of her hands and ran for the checkout, yelling over her shoulder that her dinner was half finished so she had to have it. Donna stood in the narrow, crowded aisle paralyzed with shock. This was unimaginable behavior for the North Dakota girl to absorb. What was wrong with these people?

Later, when Donna's parents came to New York to see the World's Fair, her father helped her gain a new perspective on the city. A railroad man by trade, a sociologist by nature, he enjoyed the breakneck culture of New York City. He would put on his hat, merrily wave goodbye to his wife and daughter and head out to the grocery store by himself. Forget the World's Fair. For him, this study of human aggression was pure entertainment. Looking at the culture through her father's eyes helped Donna to see the upside of the big city.

Donna slowly adjusted to life in New York and she and Charles soon married. The young couple began planning to buy a house together. Just one thing stood in their way: Charles' mother. A recent widow, she was now dependent both psychologically and financially on Charles, who had moved back home to help her adjust. Donna quickly grasped two facts: she didn't want to live with her mother-in-law, and the only way to get out of that unhappy fate would be to buy her mother-in-law a house of her own. So they did. And then the young couple started from scratch again saving for their own home.

Luckily, her job was going well. The stars must have been in alignment because she seemed to have landed at just the right place at just the right time. Working in Best Foods' marketing department, Donna was the liaison between the brand managers and the technical staff. By standing in a chasm between two groups with two different missions, Donna was often on the front line helping to resolve philosophical differences as to whether strong marketing messages or more technical information would rule the day. It was a great place for a young career woman eager to learn and be in on the action. The company repaid her hard work with frequent raises and promotions and before long she and Charles were able to put a down payment on a house in New Jersey.

Donna's burgeoning reputation did not go unnoticed in the industry. A woman at Theodore L. Sills, Inc., one of New York's premier public relations agencies specializing in food, started aggressively recruiting her. Over and over, Donna told the recruiter that she liked her job; she didn't want to leave. Finally, to get the persistent caller off her back, Donna agreed to an interview.

Within minutes of sitting down, she was asked, "How much do you want?" At that point, Donna earned $7,500 a year. She figured a ridiculous answer would get her off the hook. She quoted $10,000.

"Fine," her interviewer responded without a second of hesitation. "Can you start Monday?"

Donna was stunned. Obviously, she had totally underbid the salary, and worse, she would now have to resign from a job she loved. But again the stars were in alignment for Donna and it proved to be the right move. The fast-paced agency work exposed Donna to an unending string of new, exciting experiences. No two clients were alike. No two hours were the same. She had the opportunity to work on big accounts like Gerber Baby Foods, Procter & Gamble and the Barbecue Industry Association.

After Donna had been with the firm five years, the owner decided to let someone else take over the reins. The agency had long been run, day to day, by a strong woman vice president who would have been the obvious choice as his successor. But the owner wouldn't consider it. He said that the firm's foreign clients would not accept a woman leader. In the end, Theodore L. Sills, Inc. was sold to Burson-Marsteller, a fast growing agency that wanted to gain a foothold in consumer products marketing.

The main reason that Burson-Marsteller acquired the firm was to make a name for itself in the food industry. Clearly, Donna was the agency expert in food marketing. More than that, she proved to be the ace in the hole when competing for new business in America's Heartland, home of many of the biggest companies in the food industry. While account executives from the other big public relations firms came across as aggressive New Yorkers, Donna brought the friendly touch of the Midwest to Burson-Marsteller's new business pitches. She frequently led the presentations—like it or not.

After a particularly hectic year, Donna planned a vacation to the Caribbean over the week of Thanksgiving. She figured that the timing would be ideal for a getaway. Not so: Burson-Marsteller had moved to the finalist stage for a joint advertising and public relations pitch to Tappan Appliances located in Mansfield, Ohio. Their presentation was scheduled for the day before Thanksgiving. Donna wished the pitch team luck. "I'll be thinking of you on the beach," she told the president of the company. "No," he replied. "You'll be with us."

This was one time when Donna gladly would have relinquished her reputation as the "Midwest wonder." She did go to the Caribbean, but a few days into her vacation, she headed back to the dock at St. John to catch a boat. Destination: Mansfield, Ohio. Just thirty-eight hours and eleven plane rides later, she returned to the island hotel where her husband was waiting to finish their vacation together. It was not quite the relaxing retreat they had been planning for nearly a year, but, with Donna's involvement, Burson-Marsteller did get the new business.

Donna was clearly a rising star. And she was clearly willing to go to any length to help the business. Nonetheless, in the eyes of the executive team, she could also be one big pain in the neck. Donna often fought to get raises and promotions for colleagues who she felt deserved the recognition. One day, while lobbying the president to promote one of her colleagues, she implored him, "It would only be fair."

The president exploded in exasperation. "Where did you get this cockamamie notion that life should be fair?" he spat at Donna. "Grow up and get over it. Life isn't fair!"

Donna heard him loud and clear. She knew his position on the subject, but she was not about to change hers. She would continue to do all she could to make her world as fair as possible. The executive team would just have to put up with her.

⁓

Then, in February 1973, Donna met with the top management for her annual client review. She brought an interesting bit of news: that very morning she had become a mother. A shocked silence followed Donna's announcement. The meeting room was on the thirtieth floor. For a moment, Donna feared the executives were going to jump out of the window.

Donna and her husband had tried for years without success to conceive a baby. Finally, they decided to adopt. The process took years. Then one day the call came in. A six-week-old boy was available for adoption. Did the Myers want to see him? Did they!

Donna and Charles had to think fast. They needed a plan. They didn't have a stick of baby furniture in the house and that was just the easy problem. The tough problem was that they needed to rearrange their lives to take care of their new son. The solution was obvious. Charles had recently lost his job, and as he was a bit of a homebody, the idea of being a stay-at-home dad had its appeal. Donna had been the primary breadwinner in the family for some time. It was the expedient choice, though an unusual one for the early 1970s. Donna, never one to let "unusual" stand in her way, still had to stretch her own set of beliefs. She had grown up in an era when Mom stayed home and raised her family and Dad went out to work. Her role model, her mother, was a homemaker who had been active in the community, in church and in school. Donna had always anticipated that she would work for a few years and then stay home with her kids. It had already been far more than a few years, but, putting financial considerations aside, Donna found that she really wasn't ready to end her career. It just made sense for her to continue to work and for Charles to become the baby's primary caretaker.

Donna did, however, tack on one extra piece of insurance. She wired a plane ticket to her mother for a two-month stay. And so, after a few days indulging in shopping sprees, Charles and Donna brought their new son, Chip, home. Though Donna was high on new-mama love, reality quickly reared its ugly head. Donna had four major client meetings over the next few weeks. She became a new mother without missing a single day of work.

The fact that Donna was the breadwinner and Charles the house-husband, did draw its share of jibes. But the alternative arrangement, though well ahead of its time, suited the Myers family. Both parents reveled in their new son. Charles loved being at home with the boy and Donna continued to thrive at work.

Then, in 1976, Burson-Marsteller won the Burger King account and Donna's life as she knew it ended. Donna knew

Burger King was going to be intense from day one. She also saw it as an incredible opportunity. The first thing she did was enroll in Burger King's Whopper College, the famous three-month course designed for Burger King owners and restaurant managers. Donna decided that if she was going to market the chain, she needed to understand the nuances of running a store. And really, what could be more fun to put on her resume? She thought it would be a breeze. Was she wrong! She walked away from the "college" with a newfound respect for fast food and all that it entails.

Still, she had no idea as to the scope of the Burger King account. In addition to working on her other accounts, including one of her long-term favorites, the Barbecue Industry Association, Donna oversaw a thirty-two-person Burger King account team. Donna's team managed everything from media relations on the opening of a new store, to running complex national campaigns focusing on issues like fire safety, to determining the company's charitable giving policies and activities, to developing position papers on issues such as TV violence or minimum wages for teens. Donna faced the steepest learning curve of her career. Every minute seemed to bring a new challenge—most of which she handled from hotel rooms and airport pay phones. Donna went from spending about twenty-five percent of her time on the road to spending upwards of seventy-five percent of her time traveling. She tracked her travels and was shocked to discover that she had been at home only six weekends during her first year on the account. Her main contact at Burger King enjoyed "bantering" with her and telling her that he "owned her." She tried to smile and take it as a joke. It was no joke.

After three years, she was done. She woke up one morning and decided that she'd had enough. This was no way to raise a child, to share a marriage or to live a life. She was missing out on far too much of Chip's childhood: his first day of school, his first baseball game, his first tooth fairy visit. She spent almost no time with her husband, her family or her friends. She rarely had a minute to herself. She wanted her life back.

So she went into work that day and told her boss she wanted off the Burger King account. His face flushed scarlet until Donna feared he was heading for cardiac arrest. He, in turn, had to break the news to the general manager. The general manager, anticipating the client's screech in his ear, said that he would only allow Donna to exit the management end of the business if she agreed to stay on as the creative director on the account. Donna shook her head. She knew the position was a major demotion and she would lose her perks. She finally agreed to take the position only after the general manager agreed to let her keep all her management perks.

A few months later, Donna learned that all of the managers were ordering their new cars. No one had talked to her about *her* new car. Donna marched straight into the general manager's office. He insisted that he had never offered her any perks. Even after Donna's immediate supervisor said that he had heard the promise himself, the general manager would not honor his word.

Donna went home to think about this. How much more was she willing to take? Even though she was the agency's highest ranked woman and even though she ran the agency's largest account, each time she received a promotion, a young male colleague always got layered above her. On top of her frustration was sheer stress. For months now, Donna had not looked forward to racing off to work in the morning—a first-time occurrence in her career.

Enough was enough. She came in the next morning and resigned. She had been at Burson-Marsteller for fifteen years. No one had ever dreamed that she would leave. Her colleagues were in a state of shock as she cleaned out her desk. Donna, however, was euphoric. Finally, a chance for real change had presented itself.

~

So now what? Donna hadn't been out of work for more than a week since she had taken her first job nineteen years earlier. But the answer came to her quickly enough: she would start her own firm. Donna had never considered starting a business before. But she knew one thing: she had already put in fifteen years as a top-ranking manager at the largest marketing firm in the world. Going to another agency could only be a step backwards. The only way to go forward was to take her strengths—her reputation; her skills in problem analysis and strategizing; her knowledge of the food industry—and start the kind of marketing agency for which she had always wanted to work.

After cashing out her profit sharing and stock at Burson-Marsteller, she plunged in head first. She leased a 1,800-square-foot office across from Penn Station in Manhattan, hired three employees and opened her business with two clients who had followed her from Burson-Marsteller.

The logistics of setting up an office in 1979 were a bear. Donna was astonished to learn that just two word processing machines would set her back $30,000. And then there were desks and chairs and office supplies. She was almost in tears the day she called up the phone company to set up service. The rep asked her how many lines she needed. She started describing her business to get the rep's recommendation. He interrupted her: "Lady, for God's sake, how many lines do you need?"

The minutiae of setting up the office almost did Donna in, but once she was rolling, she realized she had made the right decision. For the first time in her career, she could manage accounts the way that she had always believed they should be managed. That didn't mean being politically correct. It didn't mean trying to second guess what clients wanted. It didn't mean putting aside her opinions in fear of a tongue lashing. Donna was free to be up front with clients about her ideas and perceptions; to tell clients when she believed they were wrong and then let them decide to either follow her counsel or not. For Donna, this approach was incredibly liberating. She felt like a better consultant and a better human being. Based on this philosophy, Donna named her business Myers CommuniCounsel, to represent the crossroads of communications and counsel.

During those early days, Donna was both frightened and inspired, realizing that so many people now depended on her— her clients for sound counsel and her employees for their livelihood. Donna knew significant challenges lay before her, especially the difficult task of expanding her client base.

But that client base started with a strong foundation. She had two accounts: the Barbecuc Industry Association and Pickle Packers International, Inc., a trade association for the pickled-vegetable industry. These accounts were small potatoes for Burson-Marsteller and often had not gotten the attention they deserved. Donna was determined to change that picture. To her amusement, she discovered that Burson-Marsteller was terrified that Donna would whisk away other accounts. Donna didn't want to play that game. And she certainly didn't want to get in over her head with accounts that she couldn't staff. So even though she sat on the board of Gerber Baby Foods, she never tried to lure them away. And Burger King was one beast she didn't want to touch.

Still and all, that first year was rough. Donna was no longer going into new business pitches backed by the name of the largest marketing firm in the world. Although her own name carried a lot of recognition in the food industry, her firm was an unknown entity. Donna had been in business just a few weeks when a man she knew in the barbeque industry smirked at her and said, "I'll bet you money you won't be in business in a year."

Donna remembered those words with a smile when she celebrated her firm's first anniversary. Within that year she had added two employees, four accounts and agreed to supervise a full-time Cornell University student intern each semester.

Within three years, Myers CommuniCounsel had eleven employees and had outgrown its office space. Donna knocked on the door of the office adjoining hers and convinced the business owner that it really would be more suitable for him to be in the office building next door. After he moved, she took over his office space. Several years later, when she was again out of space, she took 8,000 square feet on a higher floor in the same building, gutted the space and built beautiful new offices.

At that point, agency income exceeded $3 million, payroll was nearly $2 million and rent was $450,000 annually. Her agency specialized in food, wine and spirits, with a smattering of high technology clients. Her accounts included familiar names like Quaker Oats, Tropicana Orange Juice, Procter & Gamble, Chiquita Brand Bananas, Bigelow Tea, Harvey's Bristol Cream, Cockburn's Port, Sunbeam Outdoor Products, the Hershey Pasta Group, the National Dairy Board, Chinet Paper Plates and AT&T Communications.

As in any business, mistakes were made during those early years. There was Daisy. Built like a line-backer, the six-foot three-inch secretary was hired specifically to answer the phones. For weeks, no one in the office received a single coherent message. Donna finally realized that Daisy had neglected to mention the fact that she was almost completely deaf. Phone duty was clearly not her forte. Then there was Pat, a "mature," older woman who Donna hired as a personal secretary specifically to handle confidential matters. Two weeks after she had made the hire, the company's controller came into Donna's office and closed the door behind her. "You just got us into a pack of trouble with that woman," she said. The controller had noticed Pat snooping through Donna's office and had done some digging of her own. It turned out that Pat had sued every single boss that she had ever had. So Donna avoided contact with her personal secretary for years before she finally could come up with a good excuse to lay her off without facing an age discrimination suit. A few weeks after Pat left, Donna received a bill for $5,000 for a car rental which Pat had charged to Donna. No matter how many attorneys Donna spoke with, there was no getting around it; Pat had disappeared and Donna was liable. The bitter lesson cost about $20,000.

Myers CommuniCounsel also had its triumphs. There was the day the firm won the Quaker Oats account after competing with three big agencies. Before Donna got started, no one had heard about oat bran effectively lowering cholesterol. Donna's company made oat bran such a household word that the stores couldn't keep the product on the shelves. Myers CommuniCounsel was awarded a Silver Anvil award by the Public Relations Society of America for its success on that account.

By this time, Donna had been in business for thirteen years. She and most of her staff had always commuted from their homes in New Jersey, adding many hours to already long days. As Manhattan costs escalated and life became more hectic, it seemed time to improve everyone's quality of life, so she leased 7,800 square feet of space in Edison, NJ. Transforming the space into a beautiful, modern office to house the agency's twenty-plus employees was a highlight of Donna's career. It felt like her firm had finally arrived.

In 1990, Donna hired a long-time client as executive vice president to take over day-to-day management and free her up to pursue new business and re-evaluate the company's structure. Everything seemed to be falling into place. Little did Donna know that she was in for some of the greatest challenges of her life.

～

Her new executive vice president was a disaster. No doubt, Greg was a charmer. He was a fun guy, always ready with a quick line. But he had an unfortunate habit of spending most of his time in the office with his feet up on his desk—that is, on the days he stuck around the office. Greg liked to arrive early in the morning to make sure Donna had seen him. Then he was off to a boat show or a duck hunt or a shopping trip. Donna didn't know what to do. But her employees did. They gathered together in her office one day. "It's Greg or us," they said. "He goes or we go." Well, that made the decision easy. Firing the VP was unpleasant to say the least. And Greg took his revenge when he nearly cleaned out the agency's expensive wine collection. The loss of the wine was more than worth it. Greg moved to Kansas and everyone in the agency breathed a collective sigh of relief.

On the heels of Greg's departure, another senior vice president decided to leave. Lisa had been with the firm for eight years. Donna referred to Lisa as her "alter ego." But Lisa decided that the incessant demands of Myers CommuniCounsel would be too much to balance when she started a family. She left to join her family's business. Donna thought her world had come to an end. How could she possibly manage now?

Then tragedy struck her own home. First, her husband was diagnosed with bone spurs that were within a hair of severing his spinal cord. Charles had to undergo emergency surgery, but the damage already had been done, leaving him substantially disabled. Already distressed by her husband's condition, Donna now had to take over household chores her husband had handled, including the care of their four German Shepherds. When Donna's son left to go to college, the stress in the household turned an event that should have been joyful into a bittersweet affair.

Donna found herself burning the candle at both ends. She grew more tired and stressed each passing day. She lost sixty pounds. Delighted to lose the weight, she attributed it simply to overwork and age. But when fatigue was followed by flu-like symptoms, Donna went to see a doctor. When her blood work came back, the doctor asked her how she could possibly be standing on her feet. Her hemoglobin level was six. A normal count for a woman her age should have been at least twice that.

Whisked off to the hospital for three weeks of tests, Donna was more irritated than scared. She was busy. Why couldn't they find the problem and treat it already? Three weeks later, the doctors were still at a loss. While they analyzed the results, Donna went against her doctor's advice and flew to Chicago to join a client for a 100th-anniversary celebration. Walking back to her hotel room after the festivities, she began to cough. And cough. And cough. She sank to her hands and knees on the carpet in the hallway. Suddenly, her room seemed miles away. Donna struggled to find the strength to get back to her feet. Finally, in defeat, she crawled down the hotel corridor to her room. At that point, she finally admitted that something was very wrong.

Donna came back home to face an open lung biopsy. Three surgeries and dozens of tests later she was diagnosed with lymphoma. She was put on an aggressive course of chemotherapy so quickly that her surgical wounds never even had time to heal. She was tired. She was nauseated. She hurt. But she never despaired, and she never cried. She just did her best to focus her energy on getting well so that she could get on with her life.

Fortunately, Donna was unaware of the doctors' bleak outlook. She was baffled when friends and relatives called her with odd tones in their voices and talked about coming great distances to see her. She never considered that her illness was particularly severe and only learned after her recovery that no one had expected her to survive. No one, that is, except Donna. It had never crossed her mind that she might not make it. Eight months later, Donna walked out the door of her doctor's office smiling from ear to ear, having just heard that her lymphoma was in complete remission.

~

She wasted no time getting back to work. Donna knew that her business had suffered while she was being treated. Her absence, combined with the departure of her executive vice president and the loss of a senior vice president, had taken its toll. The employees tried to hold it together, but too many clients' programs had suffered and too little effort had gone into attracting new accounts. The business deteriorated to the point where it was in dire financial shape. Donna tried to renegotiate her lease to no avail. There was only one way out of the lease: corporate bankruptcy.

Donna had just fought off death itself; she was not about to let a little corporate bankruptcy stop her. At the same time, she knew that she didn't want to go back to the pressures of running a large, demanding company. It just wasn't worth the stress any more. She pared her business down to six employees and a select group of loyal clients—among them, amazingly enough, the same two clients she had started with, the Barbecue Industry Association and Pickle Packers International, Inc. She also moved the company to a two-story office that she had added to her home some years earlier. She renamed the company DHM Group, Inc.

This proved to be the perfect recipe. With overhead substantially decreased, the company immediately became more profitable. The pace eased and the elimination of a commute shortened her work days. Within two years, she had built DHM Group into a company with over $1 million in income, staffed by happy and productive employees. She focused on steering the company into what she saw as a rapidly expanding industry, barbecuing and outdoor living. She realized that her expertise in this multi-billion dollar area was unique and that it would be difficult for anyone to match the experience she had gained over nearly thirty years. Everything seemed to have fallen back in place.

Then, once again, Donna put her faith in the wrong person. In 1998, she began planning a merger with another marketing firm. The more she talked with Ann, the owner of the other firm, the more it seemed like a perfect match. Ann's strengths lay in running an office—the part of the business Donna hated. Donna's strengths lay in developing new business—Ann's weakness. After testing the waters by sharing office space, the two women filed for an LLC in January 1999.

Donna's accountant disliked Ann the moment he laid eyes on her. He dragged his feet filing the papers. Good thing too, because soon after Ann and Donna merged books, certain facts came to light. It turned out that Ann was in debt every which way; she had a horrible credit rating and her ethics could only be called shaky. At the same time, Ann became increasingly hostile. She would tear into Donna's office each morning, slam a few things on her desk, bark out a few orders and then march out the door. The situation so deteriorated that Donna dreaded going into her own office. What had she gotten herself into now?

Luckily, she and Ann dissolved the partnership before the LLC went through. The two firms went their separate ways, but not before Ann had opened a line of credit in both their names. Donna was left with $15,000 in debt when Ann went out of business.

Again, she had been taken for a ride. Donna had been brought up in an environment where people consistently followed a high standard of ethics. It was not in her nature to question, to doubt, or to expect anything less of other people than she herself was willing to give. So the self-proclaimed "Pollyanna" got trounced again and again.

Well, no more. While Donna wasn't bitter, she wasn't going to let it happen on such a grand scale again. When her father felt the need to point out to his daughter that she sometimes let people take advantage of her, she had to laugh. "Who do you think I learned it from?" she asked him with an affectionate smile.

Another facet of her good Midwestern values was the difficult time she had uttering the word "no." Sometimes the difficulty got her in trouble, but other times it actually led to big opportunities. One such break came in 2000. Donna received a call telling her she had been elected president of the New Jersey Association of Women Business Owners (NJAWBO). This was quite an esteemed role. It was also quite a huge job, eating up sometimes as much as seven hours a day. Still, Donna, a life-long political junkie, enjoyed positioning herself as an agent for change for women business owners. And it was one of the thrills of her life when, in 2001, she was honored as NAWBO's National Business Woman of the Year.

~

Donna's highs have been high and her lows have been low; still for over thirty years, much of her day has often come down to two things—pickles and barbeque. Not such a bad thing. What could be more fun than a pickle? Many of the promotional programs Donna develops for the industry are aimed at children. There are pickle tasting contests; pickle festivals; classroom pickle packages; glass pickle awards for celebrities who get themselves "in a pickle" and a fun pickle website. The creative possibilities are endless.

And then each day after leaving her new office in Colts Neck, NJ, there is the pleasure of coming home to her husband, her now grown son, her cat, her two German Shepherds and her forty grills. Yes, forty grills! So when Donna talks barbeque, she knows her stuff.

When reporters around the country have questions about the business of barbeque, they call Donna, spokesperson for the Hearth, Patio & Barbecue Association, her client of over thirty years. She conducts more than 500 media interviews a year with journalists from publications like *The Wall Street Journal*, *The New York Times* and *Better Homes & Gardens*. She is frequently heard on major TV and radio stations. Venture capitalists, market analysts, patent attorneys, advertising agencies and anyone who needs the real skinny on barbeque seeks her out.

Donna can spout hundreds of statistics and thousands of factoids off the top of her head. She can tell you everything you would ever want to know about the rise of electric grills, the pros and cons of different patio heaters and how to design your ultimate outdoor room. The one secret she won't divulge is her favorite grill. That would be bad business. She will tell you, however, in painstaking detail, the pros and cons of each model. And she should know.

She has red grills. Black grills. Green grills. Stainless steel grills. You name it, she's got it. Charcoal. Gas. Electric. An eight-foot-long grill replete with salad bar, wet bar and ice storage. In the Myers' backyard, there is barbeque happening on brick, on concrete, on decks and on rolling carts. Outdoor chefs across America hold her in awe. No doubt about it, Donna is *the* Queen of Barbeque.

FROM MISSIONARY ══════
TO MANUFACTURER

JUDY SCHMITT ════════════════
Owner/General Manager, JC Tec Industries, Inc.
Annville, Kentucky

A T AGE SEVEN, Judy Schmitt learned the ins and outs of mass production. Her line of work: chickens. Each morning before sunrise, Judy hopped out of bed and made a beeline for the chicken coop to be greeted by 5,000 hens clucking, scratching and roosting.

The first stop was the egg cleaning room. Here, she'd flip on a conveyer belt loaded with eggs that had slowly rolled down from the inclined roosts over the course of the night. The conveyer belt rolled into the cleaning room where the eggs would sweep onto a collection table. One by one, the eggs were picked over by Judy and her brothers and sisters and placed into a machine that cleaned them. Next, the eggs were carefully inspected, packed and stored in a cooler. Only after the chickens were fed, did the seven Schmitt children convene around their own breakfast table.

The chicken chores were also part of the after-school roster. Judy's mother directed her brood. Here, there were no boy's jobs or girl's jobs; there were just tasks that needed to be done. All told, about 5,000 eggs a day went through the production line on the Schmitt farm in the rural Midwest community of Jackson Junction, Iowa.

At age thirteen, Judy learned that every business has its ups and downs. The time came to say goodbye to 5,000 chickens no longer earning their keep. After the chicken business was sold off, Judy's father kept the corn crops going on their 200-

acre farm while he took another job selling feed and fertilizer to supplement their income.

The family finances took a hit, but Judy's mother saw it as a golden opportunity for her seven children. Freed from the time-consuming chicken chores, Judy and her three brothers and three sisters were strongly encouraged to get involved in the school, church and community activities that they hadn't had time for before.

Judy joined band, 4-H and a number of sports. Everyday she squeezed into the family car, a blue '59 Chevy, with her tribe of siblings—youngest children on laps—for a riotous drive to their Catholic school. The fourth of the seven children, Judy usually scored a spot on the bottom of the pile-up.

With a brother on either side of her in the Schmitt family line-up, Judy learned to be a competitor. Whether she was climbing the rafters high up in the hay loft or lying in a drainage ditch under their road to experience the occasional— very occasional—roar of a car passing overhead, Judy held her own.

Matching the boys dare-for-dare was fun, but what Judy liked best was building things. Sandbox tunnels, rabbit traps, tree houses, forts in the snow, dams in the creek, whatever the project, she enjoyed using her hands to create something out of nothing.

She also relished the moments of peace on the farm. Walking through acre after acre of corn fields. Exploring the treasures in their "grove," the clusters of trees grown to create a wind block for the crops. Relaxing in a fort in the sweet-smelling hay loft. Taking in the quiet beauty.

As much as she loved the farm, Judy didn't think it was the life for her. She never felt drawn to a particular calling, but she knew one thing: she would go on to college. Period. It had been drilled in her head since birth. Not one child in the Schmitt family ever questioned this rule.

In Judy's sophomore year of high school, she took an aptitude test to help her choose a career path. She liked math and science and the test came back with two choices: architecture or engineering. Unsure of just what an engineer did, she picked architecture. A few years later, she toured Iowa State University with her 4-H group. One of the students asked to talk with a representative from the Landscape Architecture Department. That caught Judy's attention. Landscape architecture was not exactly what you would call a hot topic in rural Iowa. Judy had never even heard of it. But it sounded interesting. The department representative told the touring students that a regular architect designed indoor spaces whereas a landscape architect designed outdoors spaces.

Judy was sold. "That's me," she said, "I like the outdoors." Her path was set. She would go on to become a rich and famous landscape architect.

A combination of grants, loans and part-time jobs paid Judy's way through Iowa State University. She loved landscape architecture and seemed to have a talent for it. She won professor's kudos and prizes in design competitions. Judy looked forward to beginning a brilliant career in her chosen field. Then her life took a different turn.

It started as a simple visit to Eastern Kentucky over the winter holidays. A good friend encouraged Judy to travel with the Ames Appalachia Committee to a Catholic church in the mountains to distribute Christmas toys to needy children. Judy made the trek and enjoyed every minute. So when a plea went out for summer volunteers, her ears perked up. Soon to graduate, Judy thought it would be a perfect way to spend a summer before embarking on her career as a landscape architect.

Judy worked the summer of 1977 in a bible program in Williamsburg, Kentucky. It was her job to drive up and down the "hollers" picking up the kids. The sisters taught religious studies and Judy was in charge of arts, crafts and recreation. She felt like a big kid. She had the time of her life.

Father Wil Fraenzle, the pastor at St. Paul's Catholic Church in McKee, Kentucky saw a spark in the young volunteer. He offered Judy a missionary position at his church. As a "permanent volunteer," the position offered room, board, health insurance and a stipend of fifty dollars a month. Judy mulled it over. She enjoyed the Christian community and it was all too clear they were in great need of help. But that spring she had to start paying thirty-five dollars a month toward her student loan. Could she really live off fifteen dollars a month?

Judy figured she had enough clothes to last a year. She could scrape by. Landscape architecture could always wait twelve months. She'd be a missionary.

Judy soaked up the Appalachian culture's music, storytelling and communitarian approach to life. At St. Paul's, she doled out food and emergency clothes, planned Thanksgiving and Christmas programs for over 200 families, organized the kids for summer camp and drove up and down steep, rough dirt roads, seeking out the elderly and hearing fascinating stories about their lives. But the simple truth was that while Judy was doing her best to make an impact, it wasn't enough. Not nearly enough.

One day, Father Fraenzle laid it out plainly to Judy: "What we are doing here is just bandage work. What the community needs is jobs. 'Feed the people fish and they will eat for a day. Teach them how to fish and they will eat for a lifetime.'"

These words haunted Judy. Each day she read despair in the faces around her. In their rural community of 14,000, Jackson County's unemployment rate hovered around twenty-four percent. Since about a quarter of the land belonged to the national forest service, there was little tax base and, therefore, little resources coming into the county. There was also little commercial activity. The biggest employer in the county was the school system.

It especially pained Judy that the teenage girls she worked with could muster so little hope for a happy future. College was simply not part of their language and the few jobs that did become available were doled out based on who was related to whom. The girls badly wanted to work, but believed that their chances of landing a job in their own community were slim to none.

The idea of moving to a different area to find work horrified them. The very foundation of Appalachian culture is rooted in its extended family network. In Appalachia, to whom you're related, where you fit in the family and what your role is in the family is largely the way you define yourself. So moving out of the community, severing from your kinship, implied an upheaval that was almost unthinkable to many Jackson county residents. It meant not just the loss of their community; it meant the loss of their very identity. Nonetheless, when poverty's bite cut too deep, many Jackson county residents did relocate.

Commuting to the surrounding counties was a possibility, but here too, there were pitfalls. Jackson County stretched out over almost 350 square miles. Commuting to other counties meant a long drive and most people feared driving outside the county. Even if they were lucky enough to have cars, they probably couldn't afford car insurance. While local police might overlook it, those in neighboring counties might not. Poverty shackled many residents to the county seat.

Judy's one year at St. Paul's quickly slipped into two. But at the start of 1980, Judy let Father Fraenzle know that in six months she would leave to finally pursue her landscape architecture career. She felt she had accomplished what she could accomplish at the church. It was time to move on.

That very same month, the city of McKee received a three-year block grant for housing renovation. When a community development office was opened to administer the programs, the appointed director of the office began his search for an assistant. He knew Judy personally and decided she was the one for the job. The director aggressively recruited her. Judy turned the position down flat. The job started in May and she had already promised Father Fraenzle she'd stay at St. Paul's through August. Plus, her landscape architecture career was waiting.

Judy was amazed when one person after another approached her bubbling with enthusiasm about the job offer. "I turned it down," she kept saying, shaking her head in confusion. But then Father Fraenzle sat down with Judy. It would be a way to really make a difference in the community, he told her.

Judy started dreaming about all the different things she could do in that position. All the different ways she could help the people she had grown to love. She thought about how tough it would be to leave behind all the good friends she had made. She marveled at how badly the director wanted her to take the position and the way that all the different people in the community had approached her with voices filled with excitement. Could God be telling her she had made the wrong decision?

She took the job.

～

As the assistant director and eventually the community development director of the city of McKee, Judy's days were a mishmash of politics; grappling with slow-to-move contractors; and grant writing and administration. Judy oversaw the construction of new roads and new water and sewer lines. She helped develop McKee's first public and elderly housing.

She also worked with a group called Kentucky Mountain Housing to build homes to be turned over to low income families. Judy selected the families who would move into these homes. At their ribbon-cuttings, she savored the joy in their faces when they took hold of their first set of keys as homeowners. The houses were small and simple, but full of wonder for families who had been trying to make a livable home out of old, abandoned school buses with orange facades long crusted with brown grime or dilapidated houses where gaping cracks in the walls revealed the green of the forest. New homeowners who had never experienced running water received a step-by-step course on Indoor Plumbing 101 when they moved into their new Kentucky Mountain Home. You turn on the faucet, the water comes out, you adjust the temperature, the water goes down the drain. No more carrying water in and out of the house. No more outhouses. No more struggling to keep warm in a house with no insulation. It was truly a miracle.

In 1984, a group of fed-up Jackson County residents gathered at Opal's Restaurant, the local eatery. The consensus: "We can't wait for the government or anyone else to help us, we must help ourselves." They rallied together government agencies, businesses and concerned citizens to form the Jackson County Development Association. The main goal was to create jobs by improving the community and making it more attractive to industry and tourism. Judy was a charter member and an active part of the group.

Over the years, Judy felt she made the most impact on the lives of the teenage girls she mentored. She drilled them on the importance of education and championed their staying in school. Some of her girls even went on to college. Since Judy never met the right man and didn't marry or have children herself, the McKee children became her children. Their successes were her successes. Like a parent, each time one of her girls went off and did the right things in her life, Judy told herself she must have done something right.

Judy's ties to the community deepened with each passing year. Whenever she saw a need, she didn't think twice, she just did her best to fill it. Over the years, she chaired the Jackson County Industrial Development Authority, the Jackson County Parks and Recreation Board and the Jackson County Women's Softball League.

Then one day a new need became obvious—literally right under her feet. Judy's office was directly above the local fire department. A grass fire broke out one afternoon near an elementary school. Since most of the volunteer firemen worked outside the county—owing to the limited jobs in the county— the assistant chief was the only one on the job. He corralled help where he could find it. That meant Judy.

As Judy and the assistant chief raced over in the fire truck, the firefighter yelled instructions over the roar of the sirens. They arrived at the grass field, fiery with red flames. With smoke singeing her nose, Judy jumped out of the truck, yanked off the hose and aimed at the fire. Nothing came out. She had grabbed the wrong hose. "What do I do? What do I do?" she shouted.

The assistant chief took over and together they managed to extinguish the fire. But Judy was shaken. Riding back in the fire truck to the station, she turned to the assistant chief. "Man, if I am going to help out I need to learn what I am doing," she exclaimed.

Judy was one of the first women to join the firefighters. The men who signed on were accepted immediately as valid firefighters. Judy was not. Many firefighters objected to having a woman in the department. But when the forest fire calls kept coming in, the chief kept on taking her along and giving her a chance. She was young, strong and unafraid; she could climb quickly up those hills. When the men saw Judy working alongside of them, putting her life in danger again and again, they finally accepted her as part of the team. In 1985, Judy was named the firefighter of the year.

In 1986, when Jackson County elected a new county judge executive, Judy knew her days at her job were numbered. The new officials would inevitably put in their own people. Judy didn't even have a moment to think through her next move when the perfect job opening came up in the Regional Community Development Agency. She could continue her work with community development over an eight-county area.

New housing, roads, and water and sewer lines were obviously of critical importance, but Judy still obsessed over job creation as the only way to break the chains of poverty enslaving her community. When she heard that one of the biggest contract manufacturing companies in the Southeast was entertaining proposals to rebuild one of its burnt-down factories in a new area, she jumped up in excitement. "We've got to put together a proposal," she said out loud. Then she slowly sank back in her chair. What did an industry proposal look like?

Judy headed the committee that spearheaded the proposal. She tapped into the University of Kentucky's economic development department to develop a winning pitch. After a formal presentation, Jerry Weaver, the owner of Mid-South Industries, bit. He wanted everything the proposal offered—and more. He wanted Judy on his side.

∽

At the factory's ribbon cutting in 1988, Jerry watched Judy closely. He liked what he saw. One minute Judy was running around in her blue jeans directing people where to set up; the next minute she was in a business suit greeting the governor of Kentucky. "That's the type of person I want working for me," Jerry said.

Jerry asked Judy to join the sales team of Mid-South Electronics, his Kentucky operation. If he had offered any other position, Judy would have happily turned him down. She loved her job in community development. But she also understood that every new contract she could bring into the factory meant more jobs for her community—and Judy was all about job creation. She also realized that down the road, the more she understood about industry, the more effective she could be in her quest to bring more industry to her community. So she would continue working with Jackson County—as a volunteer—while diving, head first, into the world of manufacturing.

Factory sales were a far cry from community development. Judy was lost, terribly lost. So she did what she'd always done when she was in over her head: she educated herself. She took night classes. She talked to anybody and everybody who would talk with her. She stayed late, often working till eleven at night. She learned the business.

Whenever Judy brought a new contract to the facility, it was her job to work with all the departments to make sure the product was properly produced. She oversaw contracts for plastic molded parts, electronic and mechanical assembly, metal stamping, welding and powder coat painting. She made sure the engineers got the prints they needed. That purchasing got the right parts. That quality control understood what was most important. After a while, Judy started to notice something strange: all of the projects she worked on had the weakest people assigned to them. As a result, she would have to learn their jobs, plus hers, in order to make sure the work was done right. Judy started to get angry. It wasn't fair.

She finally asked the manager what was going on. "You are more organized," he told her. "You pay attention to the details to make sure it gets done right."

"Gee, thanks," she said. Judy wasn't thrilled that her hard work had led to even harder work. However, the more responsibility Judy took on, the more confident she grew and the more she got to thinking. A little notion that had sprouted in her mind grew larger and larger each day. Why couldn't she open her own manufacturing company? Then she could bring even more jobs to her community. And she could help people develop skills so that they, in turn, could start more companies and generate more jobs. Instead of working so hard to entice more companies to come to Jackson County, couldn't they grow their own? Then the community could fully reap the harvest of their work.

The whole time Judy was learning and growing and dreaming, Jerry, the owner of Mid-South Industries, was watching. In 1993, the same year she was awarded a key to the city by the mayor of McKee, and five years after Judy had joined Mid-South Electronics, Jerry asked her to transfer to corporate headquarters. Judy told him she was interested; but she had to be honest, she was planning to start her own business someday soon. She wasn't quite ready yet to start her business, she said, but maybe in a year or two she would take the plunge. A year or two was enough, Jerry replied.

With some regret, Judy left her community and moved to Gadsden, Alabama as Jerry's right hand woman. Jerry shared his insights and visions for running a business and helping the community and each other. She learned the ins and outs of corporate planning and she assisted with the startup of two new companies. One day Jerry came into Judy's office to ask her to start a new operation for Mid-South Industries. "Before you run your own company," he asked, "how about taking the opportunity to lose someone else's money?"

On Mid-South Industries' dime, Judy started up Highlands Diversified Services, a contract manufacturing company in London, Kentucky. As operations manager, Judy was exposed to all aspects of manufacturing. She wrote the business plan in July of 1994, secured the first contract in September, built the sample parts in October and November and hired the first employee in December. Judy took the company from conception to a $22 million, 200-employee company in two years. And, yes, as promised, she got to experience what it felt like to burn through a whole lot of cash.

During the three years that Judy ran Highlands Diversified Services, she learned to jump through all types of hoops. There was the time that GE called on a Friday morning informing her that she had been awarded a new contract. She needed to have 1,500 assemblies completed by Monday. Judy laughed, "You've got to be kidding."

The request would seem impossible on any day, but this particular day happened to be one filled with dire predictions of the worst snow storm in decades. The predictions proved right. In sunny Kentucky, one inch of snow can cripple the state. This particular snowstorm dumped nineteen inches. But Judy had been vying for this GE contract for six months. Somehow, someway, they were going to make it work.

Judy got on the phone and called in all the staff that could make it in. They dug out an old conveyer belt and bought some plywood to put on top. Not yet having a clear idea of what assembly fixtures and tools they would need or the assembly process, she asked her team to pull out any tubing and equipment they thought might be of some help so that when the GE folks arrived with the materials, they could get cracking. The production lines were established. And they did it. Armed with just sheer determination, Judy and her team somehow managed to pull it off. The GE plant closed due to the weather, but Judy's little company had risen to the occasion.

~

By 1997, Judy felt that she had built up the base of knowledge she needed to start her own company. And she marveled that she couldn't have planned the setup for her own business any better. Even though these were her thoughts and plans and goals, it seemed to Judy that it had fallen entirely in God's hands to help her learn what she was doing before she stepped into her own business.

Now all she needed was the capital. When Jackson County was designated an empowerment zone, generating an influx of federal money designated for entrepreneurial development, Judy knew the time was ripe to strike. She moved back to the area and developed a business plan. Her idea: a contract-manufacturing company specializing in plastic injection molding and mechanical and cable harness assemblies. The empowerment designation also provided entrepreneurial training to anyone interested in starting their own business. Judy was quick to sign on.

Armed with letters of commitment from her first customers, Mid-South Industries and Phillips Diversified Manufacturing, Judy peddled her business plan to eight different funding agencies. She thought for sure they would all jump on board. Wasn't her opportunity exactly what the empowerment money had been designed for?

Well, it didn't happen that way. Several of the funding agencies said that they had to see results before putting their money in the pot. "Just how am I supposed to get results without startup capital?" Judy asked anyone who would listen.

Judy finally received her first funding from the Jackson County Bank. Everyone had told her the conservative bank would never throw its hat in the ring. Everyone was wrong. Judy not only got the loan; she received an unexpected gift in the words of Woodrow Masters, the bank loan officer, saying that he believed in Judy Schmitt, respected the work she had done for the community, recognized that she had been successful in all the projects she had undertaken and had faith that she would be equally successful in this endeavor.

Following Jackson County Bank's lead, two other funding agencies also committed. With $350,000 in funds, Judy could manage a conservative start to her business.

Judy put a lot of thought into her company name. She wanted it to be short and easy to say, but she also wanted a name that would reflect the community and have meaning in Judy's life. The winner was JC Tec Industries, Inc. *JC* came from the initials representing both Jackson County and Jesus Christ. *Industries* was a descriptor that implied the type of work the company would carry out, but did not limit her to a single mission. *Tec* was added only after Judy discovered that the name JC Industries,

JC Manufacturing and JC Enterprises were all taken. Her attorney suggested she add a third word. She selected Tec because it was short, it reflected what she wanted the company to be and it represented three key words that she wanted the company to stand for—Teamwork, Excellence and Customer Satisfaction.

She had the idea, the drive, the money and the name, now she needed a place to put it all. The problem was that there was not a single suitable building in Jackson County in which to start a manufacturing facility and she simply didn't have the funds to build one from scratch. Yet again, Judy had the sense that someone was looking out for her when it turned out the funds had just been approved to start an incubator to support fledgling companies. She was accepted as the incubator's first tenant and she was able to design her space from the ground up.

With limited funds, Judy could only afford two employees for her startup team. Her first pick was easy. Judy had worked with Lorraine Lakes for years at Mid-South Electronics. Lorraine had shared in the dreaming, the planning, the hoping as well as the praying. She had to be there to help Judy open the doors. Her second employee, her mold technician, was trickier. There were so many applicants Judy would have loved to bring on the payroll. She picked the most qualified of the lot.

Judy was set to move into the new building in May of 1998, but the contractors working on the building had other plans. Paid by the hour, they took their sweet time. Judy foamed at the mouth at the delays. She spent her days at the work site egging the workers on. Each time their five-minute break extended to a half hour, Judy started in: "C'mon guys, you're killing me. Let's get this built!"

Even with Judy's best efforts, it was October of 1998 before the space was ready. But it was all worth it at that magical moment when the first purchase order rolled off the fax machine. That thrill was matched when their first piece of equipment was brought into the building. It was a 230-ton Van

Dorn Injection Molding Machine. A gray monstrosity of metal, plastics and wiring, the machine measured twenty-five-feet long, eight-feet high and three-feet wide. For Judy and her team, the monster was a beautiful sight to behold.

But even better was hearing the clicks, clanks and clunks of that very first part—a lightening protection insulator—cycling through the machine and then finally seeing the finished product drop out on the table. The first run was small, but within a matter of months, Judy had a purchase order in her hands for a million icemaker parts. The project gave the molding machine its first full shift of work.

Judy and her team cheered every time a new purchase order came in. But the pressure was on. Judy was all too aware that she owed a lot of money—more money than she'd ever dreamed she would owe anyone. What had she gotten herself into? Could she get enough business fast enough?

Worrying, however, was one pastime she didn't have the time to indulge. She wore all of the hats in the plant: business planning, operations, marketing and sales, finance and human resources all fell in her lap. She even joined the production line and worked the machines when that was what it took to complete a job on time.

Slowly, JC Tec Industries added more employees. Judy hired a number of solid, proven individuals, but she also brought on board the people who couldn't find or keep jobs anywhere else. Many came from either the welfare-to-work or the school-to-work program. Experienced people could always find jobs, Judy figured. But she most wanted to give a chance to the people who had the need and the desire to work, but who couldn't find anyone else willing to put money on them.

It was no surprise that hiring people who had never worked before would have its own set of problems. It took patience. A lot of patience. Attendance became a big issue. Judy doled out alarm clocks and arranged transportation when necessary, but there was a larger problem at work. Her employees would work hard when they were on the job, but any problems at home or even just an urge to go deer hunting could easily keep them from their job. Instead of penalizing workers for missing too much time, she started an award program that gave bonuses for good attendance. It was no magic fix, but it seemed to help.

Still, Judy's skills as a mediator were tested every day. The gripes were incessant: "How can you keep that person on when they are always showing up late? Every day I'm here on time. It's not fair."

Judy developed a standard speech. She told employees that not everyone is going to be just like them. These differences can be good things. Those who come in late, for example, often don't mind staying late; whereas those who come in early tend to be the first out the door. "No one is 100 percent," she told her employees. "But everyone has their own gifts and talents."

Outside the plant, Judy's patience was also tested. In the eyes of many in her industry she was a woman in a man's job, a lamb among lions. What they didn't know was that Judy could be the fiercest lioness of the pack.

When looking over molding equipment in a trade show booth, she's been frequently ignored or brushed off by the sales reps. Hey turkey! she has wanted to say many times. You are going to lose the sale because you are a chauvinist.

But she's learned to hold her tongue. Mostly. And if there happens to be a piece of equipment that she needs, she'll do business. Her strategy is to fire off questions until the sales rep finally "gets" that she knows what she is talking about. Sometimes it works; sometimes it doesn't. Some sales reps still don't see the picture till the purchase order is in their hands.

Prove yourself. Prove yourself. Prove yourself. It's a near constant pressure. Prospective customers often ask her to bring her plant manager, that is, her *male* plant manager, along to a meeting. It is only when they get down to the nitty technical aspects of their discussions and Judy is still doing most of the talking that she earns her due respect.

Judy accepts that she has to work hard to earn respect outside her plant. But inside her plant, she rules the roost. One thing that she won't tolerate is shoddy work. She knows that in a commodities industry, reputation is everything. Judy's philosophy: questionable parts don't go out the door. Ever. In the last three years, only four parts have been returned to the plant, a fact Judy likes to use to shock prospective customers. This rare record demands good training and extreme diligence. Parts are checked and then rechecked before they are shipped.

By 2001, Judy was already anticipating her first profitable year. The plant was up to nine employees. The contracts were rolling in. Everything was falling into place. And then came September 11th. The blow to the economy had an immediate devastating effect on JC Tec Industries. Contracts disintegrated. The company went from operating around the clock to keeping less than a single full shift occupied.

Meanwhile, Judy was locked into a contract to relocate her company in December of 2001 to the Jackson County Regional Industrial Park, a new industrial park that she had played a large role in conceiving and filling. A palace built of steel and brick, the new building was 14,500 square feet as compared to the 2,500 square feet they had occupied at the incubator. In the beginning of 2001, that new space felt like 12,000 more square feet of opportunity. By the end of the year, however, that space just represented 12,000 more square feet that Judy had to find a way to pay for.

Then there were the people expenses. Judy signed her employees up for training classes to keep them busy over the slow period. She invented cleaning jobs around the plant. She encouraged employees with personal issues to take care of them over unpaid leave. Still, no purchase orders filled the gap. Judy finally faced the fact that to keep JC Tec Industries alive she had to lay off employees. She had faced this decision before, but never on such a big scale. Five employees had to go—more than half the staff.

These were not the kind of employees who had bonds to cash in and savings accounts to see them through the rough times. These were people who would struggle to feed their families. It broke Judy's heart—but not her fighting spirit.

Judy wanted new contracts. She wanted them badly. She pounded on doors and started looking into new ways to drum up business. For one, she took a hard look at the value of certification. Judy had heard that organizations with diversity goals rely on certification to find qualified women-owned business. She identified the Women's Business Enterprise National Council (WBENC) as the primary third-party certifier. Judy's company was certified by WBENC and she also accepted a position on WBENC's Women's Enterprise Leadership Forum. With this work, she began to see that she was a part of another important community—a community of women business owners.

Judy's business began to recover in 2002. New purchase orders did roll in. Judy signed contracts with companies who produced products for General Electric, Frigidaire, Nortel Networks, Sprint and Lexmark. JC Tec Industries also began to do work for the U.S. military.

Judy was slowly able to bring her employee count back up. The plant brought in almost half a million dollars in sales in 2002—marking JC Tec Industries' first profitable year. Judy leaped in the air when she received the year-end statement.

Still, Judy dreams of the day when she can drum up enough business to stabilize her company and offer her employees benefits like health insurance and better wages. Looking further down the road, she works hard to develop her employees so that they can someday start their own businesses and perpetuate the cycle of self-sufficiency.

But in many ways, Judy's dreams have already come true. Just about anyone who wants to work in her community can now find a job. The efforts of Judy and other community leaders have brought over 1,000 new jobs to the county, dropping the unemployment rate from twenty-four percent to just five percent. In effect, Judy has helped design a new landscape for her community. Today, hope is alive and well in Jackson County, Kentucky.

PURSUING THE ═══════
AMERICAN DREAM

NIKKI OLYAI ═══════

President and CEO, Innovision Technologies, Inc.
Novi, Michigan

NIKKI OLYAI, THE CEO of a multi-million-dollar technology firm, invokes the word *love* the way most executives talk about *the bottom line*. She brings emotions usually reserved for the family room into the boardroom. While the approach is unorthodox, she means it. More amazingly, it seems to work.

Her secret is her attitude. Her story may sometimes seem hard to believe, but Nikki is the kind of person who would say that her glass is overflowing when it is only one quarter full. True, she works 100-hour-plus weeks. True, most of her time is spent solving problem after problem. True, she is often on the road more than she is home. Also true, she wouldn't have it any other way.

Nikki was in her teens when she first started dreaming of the day she would run her own company. She had little idea where the dream started nor did she know what it would be like to sit at the helm of a business enterprise, but she did know that it would be challenging and a lot of hard work. It put a fire in her heart. And that was for her.

Status quo did not satisfy Nikki. She was always testing the world around her; stretching herself to her limits. As a young girl growing up in Iran, she took an active role in every activity. She just had to have her hand in everything. Once, at the age of two, a curious Nikki watched her mother and aunt animatedly discussing the design of a dress. Then she spotted the piece of dress fabric lying on the table. Mesmerized by the beautiful colors and the intricate, delicate patterns etched into the piece of silk, she sidled up to the table, picked up a pair of sharp scissors and started to cut through the fabric. It was such fun!

When Nikki's mother spotted the mischief, she just scooped up the little girl and hugged her. She well understood that her young daughter was only driven by her intense inquisitiveness. Whenever her daughter would exercise her curiosity about the world around her, she would simply say, "If she doesn't learn now, when will she learn?"

With parents who were quick to offer praise and slow to anger, Nikki grew up unafraid to try new things. She used to tell her mother, "Your mouth is like honey. You say the sweetest words." But her parents were equally quick to encourage Nikki and her brothers and sister to hold the highest expectations for themselves and then to stretch to reach their maximum potential. "The only limit is your own imagination," her parents would say. As soon as Nikki or one of her siblings would get to a point where they were complacent in regard to their abilities or talents, Nikki's parents would introduce the next set of challenges. An "A" on a report card was wonderful, but why not go for an A+?

No doubt, it was a family of overachievers. Nikki's father, and his father before him, had been successful businessmen and entrepreneurs. As a young boy, Nikki's father had worked in his family's citrus business. He was explicitly exposed to a myriad of business concepts from a very young age. He had then gone on to a remarkable military career. He completed his advanced military education in the United States and later attained a rank of general.

Nikki's parents wanted only the very best for their children, and to them, the best meant America. Nikki's father never forgot his years studying in the United States or what it was like to live there. He came to believe that the United States offered the very best education and far more opportunities and freedom for his children. He also realized that for his children to become successful in a new culture they had to be integrated into the country's very soul.

~

In 1978, at age seventeen, Nikki arrived in Salem, Oregon. Her parents hand-delivered her to the home of Charles and Margaret Girsberger where she would live while spending her senior year at a high school in Salem before going on to a university. The Girsbergers welcomed Nikki into their family as if she were their own daughter.

The Girsberger's warm embrace helped sustain Nikki as she struggled to keep her head above water through her first months in America. Everything was new: the educational system, the language, her circle of friends and her new host family. Nikki's studies had prepared her to read and write proper English, but had not equipped her to actively engage in conversation. During her first few days in America, people would ask a simple, "How are you?" and Nikki would look at them quizzically trying to replay the words in her mind and decipher the meaning. But her quick smiles, her earnest efforts to carry on a conversation and her expressive body language helped her to get through the rough spots and ultimately had a powerful effect on the people in her new life.

Nikki attended the Sacred Heart Academy, a small Catholic high school that her parents had picked out for her. The only non-American in the school, she received a lot of positive attention and support. Though she struggled with the language, subjects like math and chemistry, conducted in an international language, were a breeze for Nikki. She worked hard and, because her English reading and writing skills were so well developed, did well.

Nikki participated in all the usual senior year activities with her host family stepping in as her American mom and dad. Mrs. Girsberger helped Nikki pick out her senior prom dress, she poured through senior pictures to help Nikki select just the right photo and she spent many long hours with Nikki perusing college catalogs. By the end of the year, Nikki had mastered a good command of English and was well-integrated into American culture. In fact, she completed her senior year of high school with a 4.0 average and graduated with honors. Without a shred of hesitation, knowing that America was going to be her new home, Nikki enrolled in Oregon State University.

That first year in America was rich with new friends, new experiences and a heightened perspective of the world that comes from being ingrained in a new culture. But Nikki had paid for her gains. There were big sacrifices along the way. She missed her friends, her home, and most of all, she missed her family. Nikki's mother tried to close this gap with copious correspondence. She would fill page after page, always starting her letters pretending she was writing to their postman: "I'm looking for you, my postman. When are you going to come and bring me news of my little mouse, my sweet daughter?"

Her parents' concerns about their daughter being so far away were finally quieted two years later when they visited Oregon for a two-month stay to attend twenty-year-old Nikki's wedding. Shortly after the wedding, Nikki was back in school taking notes at an evening class at Oregon State University when she was surprised to see her husband, Ninos, outside the classroom. She popped out of the room before the class could be disturbed. "What are you doing here?" she asked him worriedly. Ninos reassured her that everything was okay, but said she needed to come home right away.

He accompanied her home where Nikki was amazed to see that the congregation from their church had gathered to bless their new little house. After the church members had left their messages of hope for the young couple's future, Nikki's mother turned to her daughter with tears in her eyes. "I used to worry about my daughter being without us, but now I realize that you are so blessed. Most people have one mom and dad, but you have a hundred."

∾

With her supportive husband at her side, Nikki thrived at Oregon State University. She naturally leaned toward her passions, math and science. She finally decided that she would major in computer science. Her intuition told her that it was going to have a huge impact on both society and business, and she wanted to be in on the action. After completing her undergraduate degree, Nikki went straight on to obtain her masters of science degree in computer science.

Upon graduation, Nikki accepted a position as a software engineer at Boeing where she helped develop flight control systems for commercial aircraft such as the 747. After just a year, she left Boeing to become a consultant, suspecting that the faster pace of consulting work would better suit her nature. Consultants were typically brought in when a top-priority, highly-charged project was on the table. That environment was one where Nikki would definitely thrive.

Not until years later did she consider the fact that, at twenty-four, she was pretty young to be marching into monolithic corporations brimming over with confidence that she could deliver the right results. But young Nikki never had a doubt. She felt confident that she was bringing a rare ability to her clients. She had the desire, the drive, the skills and the ability to analyze a project down to its most minute components and then articulate, step by step, what it would take to complete the project to meet the desired results.

Her confidence paid off. One of the first big projects that she was involved with was the development of the first Flight Data Recorder/Fault Analyzer on Black Hawk and Apache helicopters. As she developed a reputation as a high-energy consultant who got the job done quickly and correctly, one assignment just naturally led straight into another one. In 1989, she was made the lead quality assurance engineer consultant for a number of projects for Unisys Corporation.

As a result of working with her clients, Nikki became aware of real problems across the entire software engineering and information technology industry. It became apparent to her that few software services companies were able to successfully meet their customers' corporate goals. They just couldn't seem to deliver what was promised. When she researched the problem more deeply, she was astonished to read industry reports indicating that 98.7 percent of the software systems then being implemented were not delivered on time and within budget. Why were the results so abysmal? The reasons seemed all too clear to Nikki. There was, quite simply, a right way and a wrong way to develop software. The right way was to utilize a structured framework. The wrong way, the way many software products were developed, was to skimp at the requirements stage, jump straight into coding and implementation and take every possible shortcut along the way.

The more she thought about it, the more clearly Nikki saw what was required to build an organization that could deliver the level of quality essential to the industry. It was not just about mandating a strict set of procedures. Establishing a structured framework was an important piece of the equation, but on its own, the right methodology wouldn't be enough. She thought about what had driven her to pursue excellence in her life. She realized the key was a loving, trusting, motivating environment—similar to the one that her parents had created in their own home—that would inspire and challenge people to do their very best.

Suddenly, Nikki's dream of someday establishing her own business had become a solid vision. She knew exactly what kind of company she wanted to create. Still, at age twenty-four, she knew that the time was not yet right for her to make her vision a reality. She could, and would, continue to dream.

Her dreams were wonderful, but then so was her reality. In 1989, Nikki's first child was born. Little Daniel filled his parents with indescribable happiness. Like most new parents, Nikki and Ninos, were at the same time both overjoyed at, and overwhelmed by, the arrival of their first child. Nikki's mother came to help take care of her new grandson. She became so enamored with Daniel that she stayed for over a year. With her son in her mother's capable care, Nikki was able to return to work without missing a beat.

⁓

Then, in 1993, something inside Nikki told her that it was finally time to form her own company. Thirty-two-year-old Nikki couldn't say why. She could only say that it felt right. She continued with a full-time, on-site consulting job to help support her family. When she got home from work, she moonlighted on a different consulting project to finance the establishment of her business. And in the few hours left in the day, she built the foundation of her new company, Innovision Technologies, Inc.

It was tough enough that Nikki had to get by on just two or three hours of sleep, but not being able to spend much time with three-year-old Daniel really saddened her. It was rough. Every day was about pushing herself to maintain her demanding schedule. But her vision for her business was just *so* clear. The need in the marketplace for her services was just *so* obvious. Once she got started on her path, once she took those first steps to make Innovision Technologies a reality, Nikki never looked back. She never questioned whether or not the sacrifice was worth it. She just did what she needed to do, and each day she was encouraged as she saw progress.

To compensate for the limited amount of time she could initially devote to Innovision Technologies, Nikki was determined that each moment she spent on her company would make a difference; every step would be the right one. After years of mental planning, there were to be no false steps. So she moved with extreme care and caution.

Nikki first met with an attorney and an accountant to establish Innovision Technologies as a legal entity. Next, she defined the target market that she wanted to service, the engineering and information technology services they would offer and the corporate culture her company would embrace. Then she developed Innovision Technologies' corporate presentation. Each slide was the culmination of untold hours of research, discussions with advisors and significant decision-making. It had to be perfect. She knew each bullet point would have ramifications on her business for years to come.

A few months after starting Innovision Technologies, Nikki began the search for her first employee, a sales and marketing manager. She interviewed candidate after candidate, asking pointed questions and painting a clear picture of what her company would some day become. She had a good understanding of exactly what she was looking for in candidates. While Nikki would be working around the clock to finance Innovision Technologies, the sales and marketing manager would be required to work independently in a company that, at that point, existed only on paper. Nikki was as open and honest about these challenges as she knew how to be. The last thing she wanted was to bring someone on board who couldn't handle the unique circumstances. She needed to find an entrepreneurial-minded person who believed in the vision enough to take the risk. That person also needed to have a special way of looking at the world, so that he or she could help Nikki in forming the nurturing, caring, results-oriented culture she had in mind for her company.

After interviewing dozens of candidates, Nikki found a qualified person who was willing to take her vision for the company on pure faith. Then came the second employee, and then the next and the next and the next. Nikki had six employees and a small portfolio of clients before she was financially able to make Innovision Technologies her own full-time commitment.

The decision came just in time. In refining the equation of what would make her company a success, Nikki would frequently ask herself: Why would someone buy from little Innovision Technologies when they could get the same services from a Fortune 500 company? What do we offer that is different? High quality solutions, on-time, within budget, truly supporting the technical and strategic objectives of its customers—these things were absolutely key. But hundreds of other companies also make the same claims. What else could Innovision Technologies offer?

She finally realized that she had to offer herself—her personal responsibility for the assurance of quality. She believed that the active involvement and commitment of the president of the company would send a strong message to her clients, a message that said: We care. You are our top priority. As it turned out, this early decision made all the difference.

As Innovision Technologies deepened its network and developed a reputation for excellence, assignments came in steadily, one after the other. The company's contract sizes exploded from several-thousand-dollar accounts to multi-million-dollar accounts. It began to support Fortune 500 giants like Ford Motor Co., DaimlerChrysler, IBM and Unisys as well as several high-tech driven U.S. government agencies.

The company received a long list of kudos including the U.S. Small Business Administration's Award for Excellence and the *Inc 500* list of the nation's fastest growing private companies. Nikki was also recognized by the Business Advisory Council with the prestigious 2001 Businessmen of the Year award.

While Nikki and her firm moved to the big league, one thing never changed—upwards of seventy percent of Nikki's time is still spent working with her clients. The notion of getting senior-level attention is important to clients. But even more important than the notion is the reality—they are getting Nikki. The first time Nikki meets people, she gives them a handshake. The second time she meets them, she gives them a hug. Nikki exudes a certain something—call it charisma, call it spirit, call it heart, or call it passion—once people experience it, they know that they want more. When Nikki speaks in her Persian accent laced with exclamations of, "Oh, how wonderful!" and, "That's beautiful!" the listener knows that she is focused 100 percent on that conversation in that moment.

Nikki may have a soft touch, but she takes a hard-nosed approach to her business. She has reason to be aggressive. Back in the dot-com heyday, business seemed to flow in almost effortlessly. But as the market became more competitive after the dot-com meltdown, Nikki's company became one of many competing for the same business. Finding new business is one thing; keeping business is another. Nikki has worked hard to secure her relationships with current clients by integrating her company's efforts into her clients' road maps.

One way Nikki strengthens her client relationships is with frequent one-on-one meetings. It's a strategy that benefits both sides of the client/vendor relationship. However, because busy clients don't always immediately see the value, Nikki has developed a special strategy to help secure that time. When she wants some attention from a busy client, she asks for just a ten-minute meeting. More often than not, that ten-minute meeting then stretches into a solid hour meeting. Nikki learned this unique approach from her daughter, Danya, born in 1997. When Danya, a brilliant young negotiator, wants some attention from her busy mom, she holds up her two little fingers and asks for just "two minutes." How can Nikki refuse? Then once Nikki starts to interact with her daughter, that two minutes often as not turns into at least half an hour.

The idea has worked with her clients—and then some. Nikki often becomes so ingrained in her clients' organizations that she sits in on her clients' executive staff meetings, where the rubber meets the road, so that her company's efforts don't just exist on the periphery. They make a real difference.

Take one of her Fortune 500 clients, a large electronics engineering company. The company was told by an important customer that unless it had a third party company independently verify the integrity of its product, a safety system, it would lose the business—one of the company's largest and most important accounts. The product in question consisted of well over 100 software modules, each of which had to undergo its own set of tests and documentation. And to make it more challenging, there was a time limit of just a few months in which to turn the test around.

The task seemed impossible given the short time frame. Nikki quickly realized that the only way to get the project done in the allotted time would be to take advantage of every hour in the day and set up two teams—a day team who would then pass the baton on to a night team. Would employees be willing to work night shifts? There were no hesitations. They understood this was a big opportunity for the company, an opportunity the firm needed in a tight market. They were on board.

The precise work took patience and endurance. Nikki was right there alongside her engineers, sometimes working through both the day shift and a good part of the night shift. Whenever Nikki got exhausted, she would flash to an image she often conjures for strength in the face of challenges—that of her infant son learning to walk. Daniel would take a step, fall down, get back up, take a step, fall down, get back up. He didn't care if anyone was watching. He didn't care how many times he fell down. All he cared about was that nothing keep him from putting that one foot in front of the other. And through the project's demanding schedule, Nikki would promote and maintain the same attitude. The team knew they needed each other to help keep *their* project on track.

Finally, after months of round-the-clock effort, the project was completed. Every bit of code in the product had been tested and documented. Although dozens of engineers had worked on the project nonstop, the documentation was so perfectly consistent that it appeared to be the work of a single mastermind.

Nikki's client presented the documentation to the customer who had requested the third party validation. Just an hour later, the meeting was over. The client had successfully restored the customer's confidence and was awarded the long-term product line contract for this safety system.

~

Besides client satisfaction, Nikki gains another important benefit from dedicating such an unusually large percentage of time to client projects. It opens up a deeper connection with her employees. Software engineers sometimes see a disconnect between the executives and the people in the trenches. But, like most leaders who roll up their sleeves and work side-by-side with their employees, Nikki has first-hand knowledge of what her employees face each day. She knows all too well the challenges of sustaining innovation and quality when you are up against time constraints and other pressures. So as a technologist herself, she is able to create an environment that will inspire other technologists.

For Nikki, this environment is the opposite of the old-line command and control system of management. This environment is about leadership by example. Each day Nikki shows that customer service is not just part of a mission statement on the wall; it is a way of life.

Although Nikki offers great benefits to her employees, the most valuable perks of Innovision Technologies' culture are not wrapped up in material things. The real perks are about working in an environment that is loving, supportive and kind. Where parents can bring their children to work on days when school is out. Where a bouquet of flowers may appear on your desk when you are going through a difficult time. Where employees with personal problems are encouraged to take the time off to resolve their issues. Where the environment is welcoming and warm.

Yet there are times, as in any values-based organization, when the founding principles at Innovision Technologies have been tested. In these situations, Nikki has always been clear about what her company stands for and what can be tolerated. Just because she is gracious doesn't mean she is a pushover.

But most employees revel in the unique sense of belonging they experience at Innovision Technologies. Nikki enjoys a frequent influx of thank you e-mails and words of appreciation in the hallways. In fact, the depth of gratitude sometimes catches her off guard. One Thanksgiving Day, Nikki was in the middle of basting the turkey when the doorbell rang. Expecting to see one of her guests at the door, she was surprised when the husband of one of her employees smiled at her and thrust a card in her direction, saying, "My wife asked me to deliver this to you today."

Nikki peeled open the envelope. Inside was a Thanksgiving card. She opened it and looked down to see the signature at the end of the card. It was from Marion Chanko, an employee who had decided that the holiday was a perfect occasion to thank Nikki for her job at Innovision Technologies and to express her appreciation for Nikki's hard work and kindness. Nikki couldn't believe what she was reading—not just the words, but the fact that Marion had taken the time and had thought to have the card delivered by her husband at just the right moment. All through the Thanksgiving dinner conversation, she couldn't stop herself from continuously interjecting, "Can you believe it? What a special thing to do! How incredible!"

The card was more than a nice momento for her. It was proof that the sacrifices—the stress, the long hours, the unending travel, the tireless efforts—had been worth it. That she had built a company that people *loved* to work at. That she had made a real impact on people's lives. Nikki realized that she had accomplished exactly what she had set out to do—and then some.

Although Nikki had started her company with the idea of building a great organization, that Thanksgiving Day, she began to think of Innovision Technologies as more than just a business. She redefined her concept of success. She realized that it didn't matter how large the company grew because in the final analysis, she didn't want to be known for size and revenues; she wanted her reputation to be rooted in her drive to do the best for her employees, her clients and her community.

So Nikki disagrees—passionately, but politely—when people say that there is no room for kindness in the boardroom. That a soft touch leads to soft revenues. That big business is better business. One of Innovision's greatest challenges, in fact, is confronting inherent stereotypes against small businesses. Nikki finds that many large organizations are so focused on unearthing the cheapest solution that they fail to recognize that those cost savings might just be surface deep. Small businesses offer numerous advantages such as increased value, flexibility, quality, innovation and responsiveness that big businesses don't always recognize and appreciate at first glance.

Nikki does get disappointed at times when Innovision Technologies is automatically discounted because it is considered to be too small to compete for a new piece of business. At those moments, she tries to remind herself that she is doing her part to shatter stereotypes. With every client that receives superior service from Innovision Technologies, she is educating corporate America about the benefits of working with a small company. Sometimes, to Nikki's excitement, this lesson is made quite public. For example, after Innovision Technologies helped Ford Motor Company advance its software development capability initiative, resulting in a projected cost avoidance for Ford of approximately $600 million annually, Ford named Innovision Technologies its 2001 Small Business Subcontractor of the Year and nominated Innovision for the U.S. Small Business Administration's Small Business Subcontractor of the Year Award.

But "small" isn't the only stereotype Nikki faces. She believes women-owned businesses also are often at a disadvantage. The fact is that the vast majority of high-profile business leaders are males. Nikki believes men have the advantage of sharing more in common with other male colleagues. As a result, women do not have the same opportunity to make connections across businesses, and women business owners are not always welcomed with open arms in the "good old boys club."

In 1999, when Nikki began to see the impact of this issue, she began attending programs at the Michigan Women's Business Council. She enjoyed the sessions, but wondered how she could help translate the lunch meetings and gatherings into results for women-owned enterprises. She wanted to do more than network; she wanted to contribute to initiatives that made a real difference for the participating women. To this end, she became actively involved with the Center and then with the Women's Business Enterprise National Council (WBENC). In 2002, Nikki was elected to serve as a member of WBENC's board of directors giving her a chance to cultivate partnerships between leaders of Fortune 500 companies and women-owned businesses.

≈

Heading a multi-million-dollar company does bring its rewards. It also brings its tests. Like most Americans, the fall of 2001 was a particularly challenging period for Nikki. On September 2, 2001, Nikki narrowly missed a severe car crash in California when her business associate failed to see a red light at the intersection of two major highways and drove into oncoming traffic. The near miss shook Nikki to her core. Before she had time to recover from the incident, however, she was off to Chicago for another grueling business trip. Though she was staying at a supposedly world-class hotel, everything seemed to go wrong. Nikki was uncomfortable and distressed during her entire trip. Still in shock from the event in California, and utterly drained from her Chicago trip, she finally returned home on Sunday, September 9th to face a very demanding work schedule on Monday. Then came September 11th.

Less than a month later, Nikki was at a conference in Louisiana when she received a call from her office that sent her into a spin. One of her largest clients was considering a proposal made by one of her competitors. This competitor proposed hiring away all of the employees from the client's suppliers, including Innovision Technologies, so that it, the competitor, could manage all of the contracts—but at a lower billing rate. Picture a big fish swallowing all the smaller fish. Nikki's client was considering the proposal as a cost-cutting tactic in reaction to the plummeting economy, despite the fact that it would likely bankrupt Innovision Technologies as well as a slew of other small vendors that the competitor proposed to overturn. Nikki flew into action. She began lobbying high-level officials within her client's organization in order to demonstrate the level of commitment, experience and results that Innovision Technologies was bringing to the picture. She also had others of influence write letters supporting her company and sent them to officials at the organization. Her efforts paid off. She retained the client and saved her company.

But Nikki's problems were far from over. Just a few weeks later, after she had successfully thwarted her competitor, she learned that a trusted subcontractor had purposefully over-charged Innovision Technologies. And then, on the heels of that disconcerting revelation, Nikki learned that the same competitor that had previously proposed the "cost-cutting measure" was now whispering in the ear of another Innovision Technologies client. Again, Nikki had to act quickly to secure her company's future. She put together another campaign to lobby on her company's behalf. Again, she was successful.

Months of travel and dealings with problem after problem finally took their toll. Nikki went to the emergency room on Christmas morning with severe flu-like symptoms. While she recovered, she took a rare respite from the usual frantic pace of her life, a time-out that allowed her to gain some perspective on the past few months and her life in general. Her life was hard. It was demanding and exhausting. But she couldn't imagine doing anything differently. She realized that she had withstood many challenges and that there were more to come, but she knew she was making all the right moves.

∾

Nikki's family sees the toll of those challenges, but Nikki does have a firm rule. After working a 100-hour-plus workweek, she does her best not to bring home any of her company's problems. Her family is extremely supportive, but in Nikki's mind, enough is enough. She safeguards the dividing line between her family and her work life.

Still, as though by osmosis, Nikki's children have picked up on the entrepreneurial energy in their home. Nikki once came home from work to find her son, Daniel, then ten years old, sitting at the dining room table intently writing in a notebook. "Mom, I'm selling skateboard repair services to my friends," he said. He showed her a sheet of paper that listed the skateboard repair services he would offer. He had another piece of paper that detailed a schedule for himself and a friend who would be supporting him. The final piece of paper he showed his mother was a price list, complete with his contact information at the bottom.

"Daniel," Nikki said, excitement pitching her voice high. "Daniel, do you know what this is? This is called a business plan! You have your customers identified, you have your services mapped out and you have your prices. This *is* a business plan." She stared wide-eyed at her young son.

And that wasn't the last time Daniel would amaze his mother with his enterprising spirit. At age thirteen, he approached his parents with another idea. He had recently been reading articles in the newspaper about abused children. These articles upset him tremendously. He couldn't begin to imagine how shattering it would be to grow up in such a mean, unstable environment. He thought and thought about how he might reach out to those children. After listening to a series of church sermons on "Forty Days of Purpose," Daniel hit on an idea. He would like to give these children a "Bundle of Love" that would include all the items that might just help them sleep snug in their beds at night: a teddy bear, a blanket, a pillow, a pillow case, a toothbrush and toothpaste, and a nightlight. He thought that in the late hours of the night, these items might help bring the children a little bit of peace, a little bit of comfort, and a little bit of love and security.

Daniel sat down with his mom, his dad, and his godmother, Rebecca Page, to develop a plan. The outcome was Reach for Kids, a non-profit organization. Innovision Technologies' corporate attorney agreed to donate ten hours to help Daniel establish the organization. Daniel then gave a PowerPoint presentation, a presentation he had developed himself, to approximately 300 church members, seeking their support. The church community was deeply moved by the compassionate young man. Daniel's request for "Bundle of Love" items was embraced with enthusiasm by the church. The bundles soon became a reality.

Daniel, Nikki, and the family went together to a Head Start center in the inner city of Detroit to deliver the first "Bundles of Love." Daniel was overjoyed when the children met them with big hugs and kisses. As for Nikki, she could only stand there beaming. She didn't know where to feast her eyes: on the little ones embracing Daniel so sweetly or on her beautiful son who had just made his first big mark on the world. All she knew, at that very moment, was that she was truly living the American Dream.

SWEET DREAMS ═══════

JUDY ROSENBERG ═══════
President, Rosie's Bakery
Boston, Massachusetts

MAKE NO MISTAKE about it, Judy Rosenberg loves her sweets. Little maple cookies rolled in sugar. Gooey, melt-in-your-mouth Chocolate Orgasms. Mmmm. Delicate, chocolate-topped, almond custard. Big, spicy, jammy linzer cookies.

What she didn't love as a child was her family's morning ritual: a weigh-in on the scale. First, up hopped her father, the writer/painter turned theatrical agent, blessed with a metabolism that wouldn't quit; then her mother, a disciplined, elegant, driven and highly regarded theatrical agent with the waistline of a teenager. Last to take a turn on the scale: pudgy, cookie-smitten Judy.

The ritual reinforced a Rosenberg creed: appearances matter. It was important to look thin, to stay well-kept, not to let oneself go. Not to say that the Rosenberg's didn't believe in eating well—within moderation. Judy's mother regularly scoured the *New York Times* food section for tasty recipes from around the world for their housekeeper to whip into reality. And living in the heart of New York City, the home of some of the most exquisite cuisine in the world, Judy's mother knew where to shop to get the very best fish, the best meats, the best produce, and, oh yes, the best desserts. The Rosenbergs were equally intimate with the city's best restaurants.

Eating was not just a means of sustenance for the family, it was an experience. They critiqued every course that crossed their plate. And when a particular yummy morsel was orchestrated just perfectly, they would savor each and every bite. "Oh my God!" Judy's father would exclaim, rolling the food on his tongue and his eyes up to heaven.

In the midst of this culinary copiousness, Judy grew up with a gnawing, aching sense of deprivation. The cookies she coveted, the cakes she savored—all seemed just out of reach. For as long as she could remember, she had been on a diet. She had alternated between binging and resisting, all the while longing for the buzz, the rapture, the lust that went along with biting into a succulent, sumptuous, chocolaty wonder.

Judy satisfied her appetites in other ways. A movie magazine addict, a glam seeker, Judy grew up in a huge apartment directly below the home of Marilyn Monroe. Judy would frequently bring giggling girlfriends up to meet her idol and Marilyn was unfailingly polite as the girls gaped.

The Rosenbergs were entrenched in the theater industry. Celebrity comings and goings were a constant in the Rosenberg apartment. Their home was often full of people talking, making music and eating. Julie Andrews, Jean Stapleton and Imogene Coca were frequent visitors. The score to "A Funny Thing Happened on the Way to the Forum" was heard at the Rosenbergs long before it hit the theater. Rob Reiner attended Judy's third birthday party and she once shared a drink with Rock Hudson.

Early exposure to the theater, however, did not impact young Judy in the way her parents had hoped. While her mother and father were admiring the elegance of Audrey Hepburn, Judy was admiring the cleavage of Marilyn Monroe. At thirteen, using mustache bleach, Judy put a blond streak in her brown hair. Her father went ballistic. Dignity, class, those were the qualities her parents valued. A blonde streak? Now, that was pure vulgarity.

And it didn't end there. At age nineteen, Judy informed her parents she was transferring from NYU to, of all places, the University of California at Berkeley. They hit the roof. Though Judy's mother finally accepted the idea with faith that her headstrong daughter would someday find her way in the world, Judy's father did not. He was certain that the move out West would lead to his beloved daughter's regression into degeneracy. He offered his daughter a car, an apartment, anything he could think of to keep her ensconced on the respectable East Coast.

But Judy had started California dreaming while visiting a boyfriend at Berkeley and she wasn't ready to stop. San Francisco in the late sixties was a very different world from frantic mid-town Manhattan. In California, cars stopped in the street for crossing passengers, people smiled at each other in the grocery store and the sun never seemed to stop shining. Judy couldn't believe it. This is it, Judy thought, I've found my place.

Officially, Judy studied French at Berkeley. Unofficially, she learned that there are a lot of different ways to lead your life. In New York, she had held certain unquestioned values. Brought up in a household where self-fulfillment was emphasized more than anything else, Judy was taught to strive for excellence from a very early age. In high school, even though she rarely had interest in what she was learning, she worked extremely hard to get good grades and constantly felt a tremendous amount of stress, waking up each school morning with an ache in her stomach.

But in San Francisco, everything Judy valued was open to debate. What was the real meaning of success? Was it really so horrible to have sex before marriage? Were drugs truly evil? Judy enjoyed the questioning and the freedom to choose right from wrong for herself. Ultimately, she did align with most of her parents' values; but they were of her choosing, based on what she felt was right for herself, not what someone else dictated.

In college, Judy figured something else out that revolutionized her life: how to become thin and remain thin. She went on a 1,000 calorie diet. The trick was that she only ate things she craved, maybe a Milky Way for breakfast, a brownie for lunch, a piece of cheesecake for dinner. After two weeks, she dropped ten pounds and noticed something odd: the foods she craved were no longer sweets; they were things like broccoli and cauliflower. Then this wild idea occurred to her. Perhaps all foods weren't really separated into two categories: forbidden food and okay food. Perhaps there was a balance that could keep you gratified and, at the same time, healthy and slim. The eating philosophy that Judy ultimately embraced was similar to Weight Watchers, though she didn't know it at the time. She found it all came down to balance, a kind of Yin and Yang of calorie consciousness. She adopted a diet of brown bread, cheese, fruits, nuts and vegetables; but meals might be finished off with a brownie or a big hunk of cheesecake. It freed Judy from the constant sense of deprivation that she had carried with her since early childhood.

Her friends often teased her about her habit of ordering everything with dressings and sauces "on the side." But Judy knew she had found her ticket: no guilt—lots of pleasure.

~

In 1969, Judy graduated from Berkeley with a degree in French. Suffering from boyfriend woes and tiring of the monotony of the perfect weather, she was ready for a change. She followed a friend to Cambridge, Massachusetts and looked for work. To no one's surprise, she gravitated toward food.

Her first job was at the Blue Parrot, a hip restaurant in Harvard Square. Judy found that she loved waitressing. The work came naturally to her and gave her a newfound sense of accomplishment. After an intellectually challenging upbringing and schooling, Judy jived to the physicality, the interaction and the gracefulness that made up the coordinated dance called waitressing.

But Judy's parents didn't groove to the same tune. They called one day and talked their errant daughter into pursuing a masters in teaching. It was a security thing, they said; you never know when a teaching degree will come in handy. To appease her anxious parents, Judy entered a masters program at Tufts University. She hated every repressive and stifling minute. As a teacher's assistant, every time she tried to do something creative, she was impugned. Finally, with degree in hand, she walked away and went back to waitressing. Her parents were horrified. Were they, these New York, intellectual sophisticates, going to wind up with a forty-year-old, gum-popping waitress as a daughter?

Meanwhile, the gum-popping waitress was having a great time. In addition to her waitressing, twenty-five-year-old Judy started baking and selling brownies at a trendy art house cinema called the Orson Wells.

Then one day, Judy picked up a fine-tipped fountain pen and she didn't put it down all summer. She filled page after page with intricate, abstract drawings. She decided to take her newfound talent to the next level and enrolled in the Boston Museum School, a decision that finally brought her in synch with her parents. A love of the arts was a family tradition. Judy's father, a talented artist, had spent many years focused on painting. And most important, it was the first thing Judy had ever done that tapped into her true passion for creation.

Judy loved art school, but graduation left her wondering, yet again, what it was she wanted to do with her life. She now had three degrees under her belt and no particular calling.

Then, in 1974, a few weeks before Valentine's Day, a friend called her and suggested they bake and decorate some Valentine's Day cookies to sell to local galleries and gift stores around the Cambridge/Boston area. The two friends had a blast baking heart-shaped sugar cookies, glazing them in lavender and pink and dressing them with velvet flowers, miniature angels, silver sugar pearls and colored crystals. The more outrageous, the better. They arranged the treats on trays lined with purple satin and presented the cookies to local galleries and shops as planned, but they also approached one bakery in Harvard Square called Baby Watson Cheesecake.

The following morning Judy received a call from Baby Watson. The cookies had been a huge hit. What else could she bake? Well! Judy was an avid dessert eater, but, aside from her short stint of selling brownies, she had not done any more baking than your average American child. She had, however, spent many hours in front of impressive cookbooks lusting after color photos of forbidden desserts and fantasizing about biting into the very decadence that she'd spent her childhood resisting.

Judy went home and started to bake all her favorite childhood desserts. She was amazed that it all came so naturally to her. She had to wonder if her great-grandmother, a master baker in Czechoslovakia, hadn't passed on a gene etched with a hint of chocolate. Judy baked with a passion, trusting the instincts of a good palette developed by her parents having introduced her to only the best baked goods that New York could offer. The prototypes for each product that she created were of the highest quality. And, deep down, Judy knew that abundance was a prerequisite for enticing people. If they were going to indulge, they would not want to scrimp on anything.

So she threw her heart and soul into creating the perfect recipes through trial and error baking. She wasn't easily satisfied: too sweet, too eggy, not chocolaty enough, too many additives. And then she went beyond the treats that had so tempted her as a child and began inventing her own concoctions. One of Judy's first products involved layering her chocolate frosting recipe on top of her favorite brownie recipe. When Judy took a bite, her knees grew weak. Aptly, she named it Chocolate Orgasm. That invention was soon followed by Boom Booms, Harvard Squares and Queen Raspberries—names that became part of the Cambridge lingo. She called them all Baby Cakes and she was in business.

For the first two months, Judy worked from her home kitchen. She dragged hundred-pound bags of flour up to her second-floor apartment. Every doorknob in the place was caked with chocolate. At night, she crunched across her floor to sleep in a bed gritty with granulated sugar. She woke at five in the morning and before she even stumbled into the bathroom, she would flick the oven on pre-heat. She then fell into a frenzy of mixing, baking, frosting and decorating. While the pastries cooled, she hopped out the door to take in a quick run. Then came her big moment—the delivery.

Each morning, Judy was greeted outside Baby Watson by lines of people awaiting the delivery of her still-warm creations of the day. Sporting tight hot pants and platform shoes, with hair a horizontal frizz stretching a foot above her head and a huge grin, Judy became a Harvard Square icon. She couldn't imagine anything more thrilling.

Judy was without doubt that she had finally unearthed her talent. She had complete confidence in her ability to create a viable career for herself. Her passionate interest in food, her years of waitressing, her post-graduate year at art school, her father's artistic creativity and her mother's entrepreneurial bent all came together to create this wonderful new Judy.

~

Within two months, Judy had outgrown the kitchen in her apartment. Baby Watson approached her with a new proposal: would she be interested in building a kitchen adjacent to their store and letting Baby Watson sell her wares? Judy knew she just had to do it. She did not hesitate to call her parents and ask for $20,000. Her parents heard the fire in their daughter's voice and immediately wrote out the check.

Judy built Baby Cakes, a beautiful new kitchen in the heart of Harvard Square. She enclosed her kitchen in glass so customers could see the creation in action. Twenty-eight-year-old Judy felt like a movie star in her luxurious kitchen which was outfitted with lush cherry cabinets featuring cut-crystal knobs, an Art Deco lantern with satin shades and Edwardian botanical prints on the walls. Only the luscious smells spilling out into the Square drew more attention than her kitchen stage.

Judy would arrive at her kitchen at five each morning and work until midnight mixing cakes, yanking trays laden with hot cookies out of the oven and tenderly frosting her perfect creations. The coordinated dance she had learned back in her waitressing days helped her waltz around her kitchen with utter confidence, grace and efficiency. Now and then, she took a break from the frantic activity to flirt with one or more of the people watching her through the glass walls. In the evening, she'd wipe down the counters, mop the floor and go home. Lacking the energy even to brush her teeth, she would fall into bed. Four hours later she was up and at it again. She loved every single second of it. Working long hours felt easy because every minute vindicated her ability to create a viable business around an irresistible product; a product that had sprung from her own creative spirit.

After eight months of this brutal schedule, Judy realized she desperately needed a break so she flew off to Jamaica. For three weeks she lived in a little hut without water or electricity, surrounded by chickens running amok and coconuts falling free. She donned a white crocheted bikini, grew tan and blonde, swam in the deep blue Caribbean by day and feasted on fresh fish and vegetables by night.

As she swept the floor of her little hut, she pondered the simple pleasures in life and began to question her Cambridge lifestyle. How important were material things? How far did her ambitions go? When she had opened her kitchen she envisioned being the next Mrs. Fields, making millions of dollars by opening stores around the country. Was that really the right dream? Judy's parents lived the good life, but their ambitions had certainly not been driven by money. They were dedicated to their clients because they believed in them and wanted them to achieve their highest potential. But what was driving Judy?

Judy returned to Cambridge with more questions than answers. These questions flew by the wayside when Judy discovered, to her horror, that in her short absence her situation had completely unraveled. Years of poor financial management had finally pushed Baby Watson's managers up against the wall. They had fallen behind in their payment schedule to Judy and left her without enough money to operate. She was devastated. This fabulous business she had worked so hard to create had so suddenly turned sour. Judy regressed into the frantic nervousness she had known when she lived in New York. She didn't know what to do.

But her father did. He told her straight-up that she simply couldn't continue supplying Baby Watson if she wasn't going to get paid. So she stopped and the worst happened: the managers at Baby Watson came into Judy's kitchen, stole her recipes and hired someone else to start baking them in another kitchen. Judy felt violated. She was furious at herself for just leaving her recipes sitting out unguarded. "Idiot, idiot, idiot," she rebuked herself.

Judy didn't have much time to become unhinged. Within a month, a wealthy customer told her that he had found a space for her to set up a new bakery. "You don't need Baby Watson," he encouraged her. "You can do it yourself."

Located in Inman Square, the shop was already set up as a bakery. It was perfect. It was beautiful. Judy sold her Harvard Square kitchen and changed her business name to Rosie's, her boyfriend's nickname for her. And she was off again.

"Rosie" stood at the helm of her burgeoning business—but she was no longer alone. A through-the-glass admirer, someone who had flirted with her so appealingly, had become her boyfriend, then her husband, then her business partner. Eliot Winograd had run a drug rehabilitation program, but feeling burnt out on the job, was glad to leave his career and work with Judy to create Rosie's. Though Eliot brought little previous business experience, he possessed qualities Judy fell short on: he was an organized, regimented person who relished the task of turning the business from red to black.

The business relationship was great, but, sadly, the marriage was not. It crashed and burned after just two years. But Judy and Eliot decided to try to continue their business partnership. Working together after the divorce was rough-going at first, but both Judy and Eliot had grown to appreciate the ways they complemented each other's capabilities in business—if not in life. And they trusted each other explicitly. Judy valued Eliot's integrity; she knew he would never do anything to undermine her. With the partnership in place, she was able to focus most of her attention on the creative end and let Eliot manage the operations and financial end.

And what a relief it was to let Eliot have at it. Judy would be the first to admit she knew nothing about business when she started Rosie's. She was ruled by her passion and instinct, throwing caution to the wind as she created products that were as lush and decadent as possible. She didn't factor costs into her baking, but she charged what she felt was the highest price she could get away with without alienating the customer. Nothing stood in the way of her creativity during those early days—no business plans, no costing out, no strategizing. She was driven by pure and simple appreciation for that which is self-indulgent and beautiful.

～

Inman Square, Rosie's first location, was situated less than a mile away from Harvard Square, but in 1977, it might as well have been another world. In a neighborhood that was, at that point, short on aesthetic appeal, Rosie's pink neon sign drew in crowds. Its homey, comfortable atmosphere and incredible aromas kept folks coming back for more. At first, visitors balked at eighty-five-cent brownies, but once they bit into their chewy, chocolaty delight . . . ummm.

A neighborhood attraction, Rosie's had its daytime "regulars." There was the professor who came in each day to read his newspaper over coffee and a lemon poppy-seed muffin. Small children came in licking their lips and counting their pennies to buy a special treat. Mothers with baby carriages converged each afternoon to catch up on the local gossip and buy a pie to take home for dinner or a cake decorated for a special occasion. Doctors and nurses from Cambridge City Hospital arrived armed with long take-out lists. A plaque of appreciation hung on the wall of Rosie's from the firemen of Cambridge Local 30 who came to the bakery to celebrate their successes and lament their losses.

In the evenings, Rosie's became a dessert-destination bakery long before there was a Starbucks or a Ben & Jerry's on every corner. Aside from Steve's, a chain of ice cream stores which Rosie's happened to complement well, there were few competitors. Rosie's garnered awards in *Boston Magazine* for the Best Brownie, the Best Chocolate Cake, the Best Apple Pie and more. The buzz around Rosie's Bakery grew. Couples, fresh from a meal out or night of jazz on the town, arrived by bus, taxi and subway to sink into Rosie's overstuffed furniture and luxuriate in a decadent dessert.

No doubt about it, Rosie's was a hit. In 1983, buoyed by their success, Judy and Eliot opened another Rosie's in Chestnut Hill, Massachusetts. They had taken note of the number of customers they were attracting from the wealthy community. So when a devoted customer caught wind of the available location and tried to talk them into opening another bakery, they decided to take the plunge. Located in a busy, high-end strip mall, the bakery drew a customer base that didn't bother to think twice about the prices. The second Rosie's was an instant phenomenon. From day one, the place hopped from opening till closing.

~

As Rosie's became a Boston staple, Judy's personal life knit together. Her father saw how focused and confident she had become as she formed and grew her business. He finally was able to relax with the comforting thought that she had found her path to self-fulfillment. And Judy was finally able to relax, knowing that her father wouldn't be on her case to get more infernal graduate degrees.

And then, in 1981, Judy met her soulmate, Richard, a freelance photographer. The two married a year later. With images of a little tike licking chocolate laden bowls, the couple decided to start a family. But as time ticked away, Judy failed to conceive a child. Richard and Judy put in their application for adoption and in 1985, they brought Baby Jake home.

Nestled in their half of a two-family house, which featured a tiny but precious backyard, Judy and Richard couldn't have asked for much more out of life. Then, on vacation in Hawaii, Judy suddenly felt horribly, terribly ill. She came home to learn that she had had a miscarriage. After coming to terms with the shocking discovery that she could conceive a child, she decided to try again and at age forty, started taking fertility drugs. Two months later, she was pregnant with twins.

Judy and Richard immediately realized that there was no way they could raise three children in their tiny home. Richard suggested they investigate the suburb of Newton, near Judy's Chestnut Hill store. Judy was horrified at the idea of leaving Cambridge and moving to the "burbs." Not once in her life had she ever lived in a single-family house. But she reluctantly agreed to check out a place Richard thought she might like. When Judy walked around the twelve-room house replete with a giant backyard, images of a real family home flew through her mind. This is it, she thought. And so city girl turned into suburban mom.

Judy was so happy. For the first time in her life, she could enjoy growing plump. Also, her pregnancy moved her creative zeal to an entirely different dimension. This shift happened to coincide with another happy event: the discovery of a wonderfully competent operations person who freed Judy and Eliot from many of the duties of running the day-to-day aspects of the business.

Now Judy could begin fulfilling her dream of writing a cookbook. First, she had to take her blown-up recipes and reduce them down to size. She was fanatical about the process; working each recipe over and over until it was just perfect. But Judy couldn't deny it; it was a labor of love.

She continued to work as long as she could. But it got harder with each passing day. The growing twins were literally crushing her stomach. She could hardly keep down any food and after a few months, the thought of being in the same room with food was more than she could bear. She spent the last few months luxuriating, rosy-cheeked, in her glider-rocker, barely able to walk, but relaxing as she had never done before in her life. Finally, Maya and Noah came into the world. Taking care of twins had its challenges, but Judy couldn't have been happier as she cuddled her new babies and worked on her book.

Judy's first cookbook, laced with recipes, techniques and a hearty dose of her effervescent personality, debuted in 1991. She was deeply touched that her father, a scholar and writer himself, was so proud to see her name in print. But she was devastated when her father, who had been in perfect health, died of a massive heart attack just days after the book came out.

Shortly after her father's funeral, Judy's publisher flew her out to twenty cities where she did radio, TV and print interviews in order to promote *Rosie's Bakery All-Butter, Fresh Cream, Sugar-Packed, No-Holds-Barred Baking Book*. Though she was treated like a queen, it saddened her to part from her babies and to think that her father was no longer there to share in the excitement of her success. Judy was delighted, however, that Rosie's was getting national attention both from her book tour and from the publisher's promotion in national publications like *Bon Appetit* and the *New York Times*.

Around that same time, Rosie's had won so many *Boston Magazine* Best of Boston awards, that the bakery was enshrined in the publication's Hall of Fame. On the wings of these successes, Judy and Eliot opened a third Rosie's in South Station, Boston. It was another instant hit.

~

Then Judy was bitten by the overconfidence bug. With visions of a Rosie's in every mall in America dancing through her head, she picked out her next location, a high-end mall in Burlington, Massachusetts. After some mutual courting, the mall management called Judy one day to tell her the ideal location had just become available. It was right across from the food court and sounded like a dream. Reality, however, turned out to be something quite different.

Confident in her wonderful new store, she had refused to scrimp on even a single fixture. Rosie's sunk $300,000 into the endeavor. Then Judy and Eliot watched in despair as mall-goers passed right on by their beautiful shop. It turned out that the customers in that part of the mall, the ones who, as Judy came to describe it, dined on the "schlock" in the food court, were not about to spend upwards of twenty dollars on a custom-made cake. From day one, it was clear that the store was a horrible mistake. Judy and Eliot bailed out as soon as they could. As a friend later told Judy, she could have gone to a lot less trouble if she had just taken her $300,000 and flushed it down the toilet.

The failure set the business back financially, but far worse, it shattered Judy's confidence. The mistake was obvious: she had gone on instinct and passion and hadn't done the research that she should have on that specific location in the mall. But the mistake also marked the first time that Judy's instincts, which had always guided her toward success in the past, failed her.

Judy started to spiral down. It was a funk that lasted for years. When people would meet her and say, "Oh my God, you are really Rosie," she would just want to laugh in their faces. How could they even consider this some great thing? Judy was convinced that she would never have the expertise to make something big out of Rosie's.

Judy's interest in her business waned. She realized that what she loved was the creative birth of a new idea and helping that idea unfold and grow and impact people. But she grew weary of what it took to run a business—the constant coming and going of employees, the frustration of seeing things you had asked for a hundred times still not getting done and the worries when new competitors arrived on the scene. Judy was getting profoundly bored with the everyday grind of running a business.

She bottomed out when her operations manager and her head baker were lured away to a different chain. Judy thought her life was just over. Eliot reassured her that they would quickly fill the gap and Judy's husband dragged her away on a trip to try to rejuvenate her spirits, but Judy just couldn't get past the idea that they would never again find people as competent as the ones who had left. She quaked to think she would ultimately be the one stuck managing the endless minutiae that plagued her business. Her fear made her almost catatonic. She was barely able to drag herself out of bed.

Depression colored Judy's whole vision of her life with negativity. Should they sell the business? Who would want it? How could she possibly maintain her family's quality of life and the freedom she had come to enjoy if she didn't keep her business going? She was stuck—terribly stuck.

In the midst of her personal angst, the business was struggling to overcome the financial fiasco of the fourth store. Increased competition and rising food costs added to the stress, but the business continued to sustain itself. A new operations manager put the day-to-day routine back on track allowing Judy to break away from the business long enough to tap back into her creative well, write another book and rekindle her spirits. She enjoyed every moment of her work on her second book, *Rosie's Bakery Chocolate-Packed, Jam-Filled, Butter-Rich, No-Holds-Barred Cookie Cookbook.* Slowly, by throwing herself into work she loved, Judy began to emerge from her depression.

But Judy's attitude saw its biggest shift in 2000 when she joined the Women Presidents' Organization (WPO), a nonprofit organization for women presidents with businesses of at least $2 million in sales. Judy attended conferences and monthly meetings with peer advisory groups. She connected with the other women in her group in many important ways and she gained new knowledge and skills that helped her develop as a business leader.

But by far, the biggest impact of the group was that it shattered Judy's myth of what a successful female business owner should be. Before joining WPO, she had been obsessively comparing Rosie's to other businesses that had grown at a much faster rate. Why hadn't her business reached the heights of which she had originally dreamed? All these other coffee shops and dessert chains had taken off while Rosie's had slowly developed. What was wrong with her? But looking around at some of the other women attending a national meeting, it struck Judy as hard as a blow to the side of the head that some of these women, the ones who she had so envied and admired and wanted to model her life after, couldn't begin to touch Judy's quality of life. Many of the highest rollers in the room were overweight, burnt out, stressed out, unhappy and did nothing but work. Judy had joined WPO to work on her business, but many of them had joined WPO to work on their lives.

It dawned on Judy that the choices she had made—again relying on her gut and her instinct—may indeed have been the right decisions. In the past, whenever she had been approached by someone willing to invest or join forces, the temptation of the capital was always overcome by her fears of having to answer to someone and lose her personal freedom. For Judy, the ability to get up each morning and decide what she wanted to do that day both for her business *and* for her life was the greatest benefit of being a business owner. She enjoyed the freedom to incorporate the elements that were essential to her happiness into her everyday life: time with her children, the luxury of spending most of her day in her home office or kitchen, exercise and whatever other nourishing aspects of her life she needed at a particular time.

Through this epiphany, Judy reframed her view of her situation. Her mother had always told her that the best way to ensure personal freedom was to have your own business and be your own boss. So the fact that her business had not yet evolved into the gigantic enterprise that she had always believed was possible was not a *failure*; rather it was a *result* of a decision that she unconsciously made long ago that outside capitalization of her business would put too many constraints on her personal freedom.

Judy's breakthrough allowed her to clearly articulate another—less pleasant—reality in her life. She let herself see that, though her business had continued to roll right along in the absence of her attention, it had suffered. She had failed to continually reinvent Rosie's so that it would be forever surprising and exciting its customers. Judy finally grasped that she was the creative force behind her business and that if she didn't continue to create, there would be no business left. The business could only sustain itself for so long without Judy's input.

To this day, Judy often carries an image of herself holding a big heavy ball that she cannot drop, because if she does, it will break. Sometimes she has to fight her moods or frustration and strive as hard as she can to stay positive through adversity. She knows full well that it is her responsibility to keep things moving forward even as she deals with the changes that take place at each new phase of her life.

Judy has come full circle. Now in her post-menopausal, middle-age years, with older and more independent children, Judy has gained back some of her personal freedom. But more important, Judy has a new sense of wisdom and self-empowerment that drives her to attack, with renewed energy, the dreams she spawned in the chocolate-encrusted, second-floor apartment in Cambridge where she first baked with reckless abandon. Today, Judy builds her business not out of pressure to succeed or a drive for money, but rather out of a passion for what she does and the simple joy of creating—a shift similar to that which occurs when people finally realize that they can enjoy learning because it's about enrichment and personal growth rather than getting good grades. Judy now envisions her business as a vehicle for her creativity; a vehicle in which her role can change according to her needs. But the business can also provide Judy with an anchor that keeps her balanced, focused, motivated and challenged.

Oh yes, and proud. Today, when a person approaches Judy with the words, "Wow, you really are *the* Rosie?" Judy simply nods her head and beams from ear to ear.

~

Judy continues her quest to reinvent Rosie's. The first Rosie's franchise-like store opened in Lexington, Massachusetts. And around Thanksgiving 2002, Judy launched her new Web store so Rosie's could reach out to customers around the country.

Judy believes that someday, with the proper capitalization, marketing and skill, Rosie's could become a household name like Ben & Jerry's. But for now, it's enough to know that through her e-commerce store, people around the country are sating themselves on Judy's Chocolate Orgasms, Boom Booms and Congo Bars. They are biting into a lush sour cream streusel cake or experiencing the classic decadence of her award-winning chocolate chip cookies.

And, at the same time, some things about Rosie's haven't changed. The products are still made of the very finest chocolate, eggs, Grade A butter, sugar and flour. And in the years since Rosie's first opened, her customers have never lost their original craving for a bit of indulging, whether it be for Rosie's hazelnut white chocolate chunks cookies or its elegantly thin, chocolate wafers; its crisp, mouth-puckering, sour cherry tart or Rosie's smooth, rich, caramel-topped cheesecake. Ohhh, yeah, baby!

MARY CANTANDO is a well-known expert on the growth of entrepreneurial business. Her company, Cantando & Associates, works exclusively with women business owners who aspire to advance to the next level.

As a member of the National Speakers' Association, and a nationally recognized expert on the growth of women-owned businesses, Mary is a featured speaker at national and international events. She has been interviewed by, and written articles for, regional and national publications including the *Wall Street Journal* and *Fast Company*.

Mary is certified by the Women's Business Enterprise National Council (WBENC) and is a member of WBENC's prestigious Enterprise Women's Leadership Forum. As founder of the Carolinas Forum, an organization that supports certified businesses in North and South Carolina, she is a leader of the women's business community.

Mary is also a facilitator for the Women Presidents' Organization, a non-profit dedicated to empowering women across North America to achieve increased business and financial success as well as personal growth. Above all else, Mary serves as an advisor and cheerleader to women business owners everywhere.

Mary and her husband, John, live in Raleigh, North Carolina. They have three adult children and two grandchildren.

∼

LAURIE ZUCKERMAN is a writer and communications consultant. An entrepreneur at heart, she left corporate life in 1999 to venture out on her own and hasn't looked back since. Laurie works with businesses that range from startup companies to Fortune 500 corporations to help them communicate their stories. She also contributes columns and feature articles to a number of business journals. This is Laurie's first book.

Laurie lives in Chapel Hill, North Carolina with her husband, Josh, their baby, Yana, and their two golden retrievers.

Have you faced challenges and landed on your feet?

*"As women, we must share our stories.
This is what seeds our imaginations."*

We are looking for more stories about remarkable women business owners. If you or someone you know would like to be considered for our next book, please go to www.WomanBusinessOwner.com and complete the online questionnaire.

∾

To purchase copies of this book, visit
www.WomanBusinessOwner.com